The Productive Models

Also by Robert Boyer

REGULATION THEORY: THE STATE OF ART (*co-editor with Yves Saillard*)

JAPANESE CAPITALISM IN CRISIS (*co-editor with T. Yamada*)

BETWEEN IMITATION AND INNOVATION. THE TRANSFER AND HYBRIDIZATION OF PRODUCTIVE MODELS IN THE INTERNATIONAL AUTOMOBILE INDUSTRY (*co-editor with Elsie Charron, Ulrich Jürgens, Steven Tolliday*)

CONTEMPORARY CAPITALISM: THE EMBEDDEDNESS OF INSTITUTIONS (*co-editor with R. Hollingsworth*)

AFTER FORDISM (*with Jean-Pierre Durand*)

STATES AGAINST MARKETS: THE LIMITS OF GLOBALIZATION (*co-editor with Daniel Drache*)

THE RETURN TO INCOMES POLICY (*co-editor with Ronald Dore, Z. Mars*)

THE REGULATION SCHOOL. A CRITICAL INTRODUCTION

THE SEARCH FOR LABOUR MARKET FLEXIBILITY

Also by Michel Freyssenet

ONE BEST WAY? TRAJECTORIES AND INDUSTRIAL MODELS OF THE WORLD'S AUTOMOBILE PRODUCERS (*co-editor with Andrew Mair, Koichi Shimizu, Giuseppe Volpato*)

The Productive Models
The Conditions of Profitability

edited by

Robert Boyer
National Center of Scientific Research, Paris
GERPISA International Network

and

Michel Freyssenet
National Center of Scientific Research, Paris
GERPISA International Network

translation from French by
Alan Sitkin

in association with

GERPISA

Réseau International
International Network
Groupe d'Etude et de Recherche Permanent sur l'Industrie et les Salariés de l'Automobile
Permanent Group for the Study of the Automobile Industry and its Employees
Ecole des Hautes Etudes en Sciences Sociales, Paris, Université d'Evry-Val d'Essonne

First published 2000 in France by Editions la Decouverte, Paris,
as *Les Modèles Productifs*

This edition published 2002 by
PALGRAVE MACMILLAN
Houndmills, Basingstoke, Hampshire RG21 6XS and
175 Fifth Avenue, New York, N.Y.10010
Companies and representatives throughout the world

PALGRAVE MACMILLAN is the new global academic imprint of the Palgrave
Macmillan division of St. Martin's Press, LLC and of Palgrave Macmillan Ltd.
Macmillan© is a registered trademark in the United States, United Kingdom
and other countries. Palgrave is a registered trademark in the European
Union and other countries.

ISBN 1—4039—0072—8

This book is printed on paper suitable for recycling and made from fully
managed and sustained forest sources.

A catalogue record for this book is available from the British Library.

Library of Congress Cataloging-in-Publication Data
Quel modèle productif? English
     The productive models / Robert Boyer, Michel Freyssenet.
        p. cm.
     Includes bibliographical references and index.
     ISBN 1-4039-0072-8
       1. Automobile industry and trade—Japan. 2. Automobile industry
     and trade—United States. 3. Automobile industry and trade—Europe.
     I. Boyer, Robert, 1943– II. Freyssenet, Michel. III. Title.

     HD9710.J32 Q4413 2002
     658.4'01—dc21
                                                                    2002025190

10   9   8   7   6   5   4   3   2   1
11   10   09   08   07   06   05   04   03   02

Printed and bound in Great Britain by
Antony Rowe Ltd, Chippenham and Eastbourne

Contents

List of Tables

List of Figures

List of Abbreviations

CEO	Chief Executive Officer
CVCC	Compound Vortex Controlled Combustion
FRG	Federal Republic of Germany
GATT	General Agreement on Tariffs and Trade
GM	General Motors
GERPISA	Groupe d'Étude et de Recherche Permanent sur l'Industrie et les Salariés de l'Automobile, permanent group for the study of the automobile industry and its employees (see appendix)
ICT	Information and Communication Technologies
IMVP	International Motor Vehicle Programme
MIT	Massachusetts Institute of Technology
MITI	Ministry of International Trade and Industry
NUMMI	New United Motor Manufacturing
OECD	Organisation for Economic Co-operation and Development
SUVs	Sport Utility Vehicles
TMM	Time and Motion Method
UAW	United Automobile Workers

Preface

Over the next few decades, will 'lean production' and a generalised deregulation of trade have become the norms for the international environment in which firms and political and economic spaces will be operating?

The GERPISA Group, a French-based permanent research network that is devoted to the study of the automobile industry and its labour force, has been transformed into an international network of researchers whose backgrounds cover a wide range of social sciences (economics, business, history, sociology, geography, and political science). From 1993 to 1996, the Group carried out an initial international programme entitled 'The Emergence of New Industrial Models', a project in which it examined whether existing industrial models were effectively starting to converge towards the principles of 'lean production' – as had been theorised by MIT's IMVP team. By focusing on what was happening in the automobile industry, the GERPISA Group's work was able to demonstrate the great diversity, and divergence, of the trajectories that firms have been following in recent times. Examples have been the wide spectrum of product policies; of productive organisations and labour relations; and the hybridisation of production systems in the new spaces towards which firms have been expanding.

The participants reached the shared conclusion that both theoretically and in practice there have been, there remains today, and there will probably be tomorrow, several successful productive models. The reasoning behind this conclusion is presented and discussed in the four collective books produced by the four working groups, which represent different elements of the integrated project: Freyssenet, M., Mair, A., Shimizu, K., Volpato, G. (eds.), *One Best Way? Trajectories and Industrial Models of the World's Automobile Producers*, Oxford University Press, Oxford, 1998; Boyer, R., Charron, E., Jürgens, U., Tolliday, S. (eds.), *Between Imitation and Innovation. The Transfer and Hybridization of Productive Models in the International Automobile Industry*, Oxford University Press, Oxford, 1998; Durand, J. P., Stewart, P., Castillo, J. J. (eds.),*Teamwork in the Automobile Industry. Radical Change or Passing Fashion*, Macmillan, London, 1999; Lung, Y., Chanaron, J. J., Fujimoto, T., Raff, D. (eds.), *Coping with Variety: Product Variety and Production*

Organization in the World Automobile Industry,   Ashgate, Aldershot, 1999.

Each book has its own particular focus, but all explain the plurality of productive models. The thesis of convergence towards a single model is based on the idea that success comes from combining methods which appear to give the best results, assuming that the environment is largely common to all firms. But reality suggests otherwise. Successful techniques are so only under certain economic and social conditions. Although growing liberalisation of international trade and economic deregulation in many countries may have led to a convergence in competitive conditions, others factors are creating fresh sources of differentiation in both demand and costs structure. Indeed productive models emerge from these partly unintended processes which result in coherence between strategies, organisation forms and practices, and the fit between these and the economic and social environment. It is the process of achieving internal coherence and external fit which makes companies successful.

While the members of GERPISA reached agreement on these conclusions, they did not reach agreement on precisely how to characterise the various models. Time and resources did not permit full development of the debates, and, therefore, the contributors to the four books have adopted their own characterisations of productive models, leaving the door open to further theoretical in this area. The scientific directors of the programme, Robert Boyer and Michel Freyssenet, went on the work. They enhanced it by findings from research on the automobile industry since its birth and by some results of the second international programme of GERPISA, 'The Automobile Industry, between Globalisation and Regionalisation'. In the present book, they expose their main conclusions. They propose an analytical framework to explain the renewed diversity of productive models. They characterise each of them as a company governance compromise between the main players, which have to find coherent means with one of the viable profit strategies in the economic and social context of the company. In a further book, *The World that Changed the Machine*, they will attempt to explain the history of automobile industry through the processes of emergence, development, diffusion and crisis of the identified productive models in the different national growth modes.

GERPISA' s books are not only the result of the work done by their authors. Through their participation in the international meetings, and in the annual symposiums, the members of the programme's international steering committee, and all the others members of the network, have contributed to various degrees to the discussions, and to the general thought process. In addition, the books would have never seen the day had it not been for GERPISA's administrative staff, who take care of the tasks that are part of the daily life of an international network. We thank them all.

GERPISA International Network

1
Introduction

During the 1990s, many scientific publications, economic manuals and mass media pundits held that a correct representation of the industrial history of the 20th century would break this period down into three phases. The first phase was thought to involve 'semi-craft' production, characterised by a wide variety of goods made by self-organised professional workers seeking to satisfy a demand that emanated from the upper social categories, these being the only persons who could access such custom-made items.

Then came a phase of 'mass production', characterised by the manufacturing of large series of standardised goods by unskilled workers whose efforts were strictly defined and prescribed. Thanks to the economies of scale that were made possible by this system, it was supposedly during this period that the working classes acceded to a consumption of industrial products.

Lastly, the century's third and final phase of productive activity, called 'lean production', was said to have appeared in the 1990s, first in Japan before diffusing across the rest of the world. This system was said to have enabled a manufacturing of diversified, high-quality and competitively priced goods, thanks to employees' and suppliers' joint efforts towards a continuous improvement in performance (the purpose being to satisfy a market that was becoming increasingly competitive and globalised). This final phase was said to have signalled the end of the so-called Taylorian division of labour, assimilated with a separation of design and execution.

The MIT (Massachusetts Institute of Technology) researchers put together an International Motor Vehicle Programme (IMVP) to direct research into automobile manufacturer and variation within their levels of productivity. It subsequently devised the lean production theory to account for the system of production it was describing. The IMVP stated that this system 'would change the world', and that it was imperative that American and European firms adopt it (Womack et. al., 1990).

This thesis, which was widely successful internationally in both professional and scientific circles, nevertheless raised a greater number of questions, and even outright criticism. This in turn led to a new wave of research throughout the 1990s – initiatives that enabled more operative types of theoretical formulation. The purpose of the present book is to present these latter formulations.

History however moves quickly. The 'system that was going to change the world' was not able to keep the country where it was said to have originated from going into a protracted and painful crisis. Nor did it prevent some of the companies who allegedly embodied its principles from being forced to ally themselves with (or even be taken over by) foreign groups – only to be restructured and discover that they had much to learn from foreigners who were reputedly less efficient. Methods that had been attributed to the Japanese and which had seduced economic and political leaders (as well as many university professors and researchers) began to lose their charm.

One intellectual fashion replacing another, now a new 'Anglo-Saxon' model, based on the search for short-term profitability and a consequence of the power that has been acquired by institutional investors (pension funds, mutual funds, etc.) is supposedly forcing itself on the rest of the planet – just as 10 years ago people had been saying that lean production was sure to be the way of the future. The disillusion is as blinding as it is fascinating. It makes it difficult to learn from the past and causes analysts to repeat the same mistakes – notably those which consist of seeing a new phenomenon as a potentially general and irreversible tendency without first examining the conditions that led to its birth or which are necessary if it is to spread.

It is crucial that analysts avoid falling prey to faddish thinking again, whatever the nature thereof. Observers have to engage in conceptual clarifications and carry out meticulous analyses. This has been the goal of the 'GERPISA International Network' (permanent group for the study of the automobile industry and its employees [see appendix]), an association of researchers who have been focusing on the automobile industry in an attempt to verify the validity of the IMVP's thesis. GERPISA has been studying automobile firms' trajectories as well as the spaces in which such companies have deployed their activities from the late 1960s through the late 1990s. This has been achieved via two international research programmes: '*The emergence of new industrial models*' (1993–1996) and '*The automobile industry between globalisation and regionalisation*' (1997–1999).

The authors of the present book, who managed the scientific aspects of these two programmes, present here the conclusions that they have personally drawn from them, enhanced by findings from research into the automobile industry since its birth. The present book provides an analytical structure that could readily inspire research into other sectors of activity. For the moment, the automobile sector is the only one to have been subjected to systematic investigation at a worldwide level.

The stakes are high in this debate. At a scientific level, they involve an understanding of the full diversity of the various forms that the relationship between capital and labour has assumed, wherever this relationship is being renewed on a daily basis (i.e., in those firms and economic and political spaces where such activities are deployed). At a practical level, we focus on the conditions underlying firms' durable profitability (and thus longevity), thereby assessing the room to manoeuvre for each of the players involved: shareholders, banks, executives, employees, labour unions, suppliers, the State and local authorities – with consideration being given to each participant's own economic and social outlook.

The second chapter of the present book suggests a framework for analysing the process that gives birth to a 'productive model'. The purpose is to build a definition that can be used operationally. The six following chapters are devoted to the 'profit strategies' that can become possible, depending on the state of the market and labour; and to the 'productive models' by which these strategies (such as they have been defined up until now in the automobile industry) can be implemented. Each chapter presents the development of one (or two) productive model(s); the profit strategy it implements; the means it activates; the 'company governance compromise' in which it is embedded; the firms that have successfully embodied it (and those who have failed); the crises it has known; and finally the future that can be predicted for it. The conclusion (chapter 9) provides an overview of the way in which these productive models have evolved over time, and specifies both the conditions in which firms can be profitable as well as the room for manoeuvre that participants have at their disposal.

2
Engendering productive models: an analytical framework

Productive models have spawned at least three major debates amongst social scientists. The first relates to the criteria that make it possible to distinguish amongst such models; the second to their singular or pluralistic nature; and the third to their universality or their embeddeness in a given context. A good way to broach these issues would be to remind ourselves of the main challenges firms face. This will allow us to reconstitute the processes that cause them to make strategic choices in order to become profitable, or to acquire resources that they can implement.

Two basic types of obligations and uncertainties

In the 18th century, Europe established the freedom to buy and sell not only goods and services but also the individual and collective capacities for realising them. This created competition between firms and between individuals; transformed the businesses affected into wage earning activities; and transmogrified the means allocated towards this end into a return-seeking type of capital investment. Amongst a whole slew of social relationships, this new freedom led to one that was generally called the 'capital and labour relationship', and which has since become a predominant form. The loosening of the constraints and prohibitions that had been imposed on the economy by the previous system of professional guilds and feudal and royal prerogatives (which had affected both the owners of the means of production as well as their workers) was offset by a twofold obligation and a double uncertainty: the obligation that all capital invested be profitable and that every wage earner accept geographic and professional mobility; and market uncertainty as to the actual selling of the goods and services on offer plus labour uncertainty as to the feasibility of producing such goods and services under the required conditions (Freyssenet, 1999b).

All invested capital is in fact obliged, over the medium term, to generate a profit that is at least equal to average rates of profit – otherwise it will one day be subject to competition, elimination or absorption by more profitable units. Hence the unending search for new markets, sources of profit, products and means of production. As for workers, they have been forced to develop and even change their competencies so that they can become purchasable commodities for employers and be shifted back and forth (depending on the location of capital). The result is a considerable acceleration both in technical change and also in a professional and geographic mobility that has been historically manifested by the major upheavals that periodically revolutionise industry as well as the space(s) in which it operates. Hence the sentiment that there have been a succession of industrial revolutions.

These obligations have lead to a considerable extension of the market place and of the division of labour. With society becoming increasingly focused on wage earning, product markets depend more and more on the income that employees derive from the sale of their working capacities.

Yet nothing guarantees with certainty that those who are investing their capital will find clients to purchase the products being manufactured. Nor are they sure to obtain in all circumstances from their employees the output that they desire (on time, with good quality and at a low cost), since this will depend on employees' competence and on individual and collective acceptance of labour relations, rights and usual practices

Paths that could theoretically lessen market and labour-related uncertainties

There are several ways to reduce market uncertainty:
- The first consists of determining as far as this is possible the extent to which solvent demand actually exists. It also involves acquiring a durable competitive advantage, given the priorities that the potential buyers may have (price, quality, diversity, novelty, availability, etc.). Competitive advantage can include wages, products, means of production, organisation etc. It can also be common to firms in a given country, with the public authorities ensuring corporate competitiveness in the international market place and attracting foreign firms into the country via an advantageous tax system, favourable

exchange rates, an efficient infrastructure, a well-trained labour force, support for technological innovation, etc.

- The second is to act on the source and distribution of national income, in other words, on the 'growth mode'. The purpose is to increase the predictability of quantitative and qualitative variations in demand, and to limit the number of areas where there is competition between firms and between employees. This is a type of capitalism that has been organised in such a way as to respect macro-economic and social equilibrium. For instance, by adopting a nationally co-ordinated and moderately hierarchised distribution of income during the post-war boom years, a number of industrialised countries provided their firms with a good visibility of the volume and structure of future demand.

Countries, like firms, are not free to choose between these two major paths towards reduced market uncertainty. The ability to reach this goal depends specifically on each country's mode of international insertion, and on its sources of growth.

To reduce labour uncertainty, there are also two paths that can be followed:

- either establish a contract of lasting trust with wage earners, granting them the power to co-operate and to share their know-how on the condition that they agree to help improve products, production techniques and the firm's performances (in exchange for a compensation that can be negotiated);
- or else to restrict, through the preparation and prescription of work, employees' freedom to evaluate things themselves – this being a strength they may otherwise use to gain advantages, de facto power or rights that are judged by the possessors of capital to be contradictory to the firm's mission and objectives. Here the division of labour becomes a division of the intelligence of labour.

Although there have been a number of oscillations between these two paths, there is no question but that the second one has dominated historically, as witnessed by the various and successive technical and organisational choices that have been made in all of those sectors of activity and countries that capitalism has reached – to such a point that the first path seems 'unrealistic' and contrary to industrial 'modernity'.

All in all, market and labour uncertainty can be managed at two different levels:

- at the level of the economic and political space that has been set up (generally a national space but sometimes a world 'region'), through the establishment of a 'growth mode',

---

The division of the intelligence of labour

This consists of designing production processes, machines, work organisations and forms of co-operation between employees in such a way as to restrict the activities of those employees who will be implementing this process – in other words, by pre-determining its substance (total prescription being something that is unfeasible).

There is nothing new about attempts to materialise human intelligence in a tool that increases adaptation to the goal being pursued. This can be observed in all societies. However, the process has been used towards a variety of different ends, and takes on specific forms depending on the dominant social relationship. Labour 'freedom' and the uncertainty that goes along with it have lead to productive techniques which tend to transform employees into appendages of their machines (whether or not the work involves a realisation of physical or mental operations, or else a supervision of indicators and an application of procedures) instead of turning machines into tools that help to deploy people's individual capabilities (except for that part of the design that has not yet been divided).

This materialisation process cannot reach its goal immediately, nor is it ever completed. Above and beyond the fact that it engenders costly dysfunctions in the new techniques' finalisation phase (the division of the intelligence of labour makes it impossible to anticipate with any efficiency all of the potential productive situations), it also affects whatever skilled work was inherited from the previous division of the intelligence of labour. For the capitalist, a modicum of intelligence is therefore always left over, hence uncertainty that must be managed on a day-to-day basis. It is this subsection that is subject to a greater or a lesser division, depending on the work organisation that has been chosen (Freyssenet, 1974, 1997).

- at the level of the individual firm, through the choice of a 'profit strategy' that takes into account market and labour characteristics – and through the building of a 'productive model' that can implement this profit strategy.

`Growth modes´

These are characterised by a main source of national income and by a form of distribution for this income. Depending on the way in which they are combined, market and labour uncertainties are not all the same. As a result, the conditions in which firms can make profits also differ (Aglietta, 1976: Boyer, Mistral, 1978; Boyer 1988; Boyer, Saillard, 2001).

Sources of national income and forms of distribution

Growth in national income can be primarily 'driven' by investments, by domestic consumption or by exports. In the first instance, a large percentage of the income created is reallocated to the production of the infrastructure and of the means of production or destruction. Where consumption is a priority, growth originates from a national income distribution that encourages greater purchasing power for all or part of the population. In this situation, growth is based on the productivity gains that have been achieved in a given space. Where growth is driven by the export of raw materials, agricultural products or industrial goods or services, its rhythm depends on world prices (for the first two motives), or else on price competitiveness and/or degree of specialisation for the latter. There is no doubt that growth in all countries is nurtured by all three sources, but in reality one source usually dominates. This depends on a country's resources, the developmental phase in which it finds itself, its international positioning, industrial history and national political compromise.

Four main forms of income distribution were observed during the 20th century:

- A 'competitive' form of distribution prevailed in many industrial countries during the first half of the century, and has recently reappeared in certain countries. This form is a function of the balance of power at a local and category-specific level, and depends on financial, ownership-related and commercial opportunities.
- 'Shortage-related' distribution forms cropped up during the 1920s and persisted after the Second World War in certain countries involved in a rebuilding process (or for a longer period of time in countries with a Soviet type of economy). This is a typical distribution form for eras marked by political, military or economic mobilisation. It goes hand-in-hand with investment as a (main) source of growth.
- A 'nationally co-ordinated and moderately hierarchised' form of distribution was an attribute of most so-called Western countries (including Japan) except Great Britain, from the 1950s until the early 1980s. Political, economic and social partners would periodically get together to discuss how increases in total wages could correspond to mutually acceptable macroeconomic criteria. They would also discuss income disparities and ensure that the pyramid remained relatively flat, notably through fiscal measures and transfer policies.
- An 'inegalitarian' form of distribution has above all persisted in certain formerly colonised countries where an initially land-based

oligarchy has been able to renew the economic and political foundations of its power. As such, this form exists to benefit social categories comprised of (land)owners and other leaders, only redistributing a small proportion of income to the dependent social classes, and emphasising vote-catching postures.

There are fewer growth modes than there are combinations of income sources and forms of distribution. Eight main varieties could be counted during the course of the 20th-century. The relevant space in which firms have been deciding upon their profit strategy and building up their productive model has therefore been neither a (so-called) unified global space – nor a specific and unique national one.

Eight growth modes that shaped the market and labour during the 20th century

By convention, growth modes are first labelled by the specific form of income distribution which they represent, and then by the main source of this income (table 2.1).

- A 'competitive and competed' mode could be found in most European countries before the First World War. It remained the dominant mode for certain countries in this group during the interwar period. It has continued to be Great Britain's de facto mode until today, with the exception of a short period straddling the 1960s and 1970s. It constitutes the theoretical horizon of liberalised global trade. Exposed to free trade, those countries that have adopted this mode experience a type of growth whose rhythm matches variations in firms' competitive positions, both in the domestic and in the export markets. National income distribution reflects the balance of power at a local and professional level as well as financial opportunism – with 'external constraints' and the risk of bankruptcy ultimately playing a regulator's role for all. One after the other, all firms and employees become competitors as well as targets of competition. Not only is the market limited because of this state of affairs, it also becomes unstable and economically and socially compartmentalised, reaching in certain instances a balkanised status. As for labour, it is both flexible and fragmented: flexible because high inter-firm mobility maximises wages where the labour market allows for this (given the uncertain nature of future outcomes) – and fragmented because professional groups, in anticipation of harder times, organise themselves when they are capable of doing so in such a way as to obtain or defend (each independently of the other) the autonomy and advantages they have gained.

- A 'competitive and consumer-oriented' mode is characterised by a type of growth that is driven by domestic consumption and competitive distribution. This mode prevailed in the United States until the Second World War, and in certain European countries during the interwar period. The United States went back to this mode in the 1980s, attempting to deregulate the last sectors where income distribution was still carried out on a 'nationally co-ordinated' basis. Consumption-based growth generates a more stable and broader type of demand than the preceding mode, but competitive distribution tends to restrict its extension to the average, independent and/or wage earning social categories. It also tends to provoke the emergence of new expectations from those social groups within the general population that have either benefited from the competitive framework or else been penalised by it. The economies of scale that are enabled by this mode engender a division of labour, bringing with it a change in the structure of the workforce. Professional guilds are replaced by branch-wide unions. It is easier to organise work and create solidarity between various category-specific and national levels than to limit competition between wage earners.

- A 'competitive and price export-oriented' mode has characterised certain Asian countries since the 1970s. These countries are either totally lacking in resources, or else possess very few. On the other hand, they are richly endowed with a well-trained workforce and open to foreign investors. Moreover, for very specific historical and geo-strategic reasons (i.e., 'socialist containment' policies), they have been basically involved in one-sided export activities, first sending industrialised countries cheap bottom-of-the-range products, and later more sophisticated goods that could be sold at very competitive prices. Certain countries (i.e., South Korea) have deliberately tried to use the international situation in such a way as to build up a purely national industry, notably in the automobile sector, whilst methodically organising the indispensable technology transfers.

- A 'co-ordinated and consumer-oriented' growth mode characterised the United States from the 1940s until the early 1980s, and France and Italy from the 1950s until the mid-1980s. This mode featured a consumption-driven growth that could be extended and developed due to a nationally co-ordinated and moderately hierarchised distribution of productivity gains that took on the form of increases in the purchasing power of wages. Factors such as a generalised rise in living standards, a moderate and stabilised hierarchisation of income and upwards social mobility engendered a mass market for household equipment whose hallmark was the gradual nature of its hierarchy (i.e., it lacked in any major discontinuities between its various segments). Work was organised into powerful branch-wide and national labour unions that became indispensable partners in the income setting process. The different work statuses ensured both stable employment and income security, during the population's working life as well as afterwards.

- A 'co-ordinated and specialised export-oriented' mode was characteristic of Germany from the 1950s until the late 1990s and of Sweden also from the 1950s until the late 1980s. Although Sweden's income distribution mode has since gone into a major crisis, Germany has to a large degree been able to preserve its variant. National growth in this mode is based on exporting goods and services that are sufficiently specialised to avoid being subjected to price-based competition. National income distribution reflects the gains that are derived from this competitiveness. It is co-ordinated nationally and barely hierarchised, meaning that domestic consumption amplifies growth. This in turn stimulates investment. The market to which this type of mode lends itself is moderately hierarchised and dominated by middle and upper social segments as a result of the high wage levels that are being paid. Work is characterised by very stable employment, a large percentage of skilled workers, co-operative yet powerful labour unions, and advanced social protection systems.
- A 'co-ordinated and price export-oriented' growth mode is driven by exports of price competitive mundane products. The nationally co-ordinated and moderately hierarchised distribution of income reflects export performances. This was Japan's mode, and to a large extent it was still in place in that country in 2000. As in the preceding example, domestic consumption and investment benefit from the knock-on effect of export success. The domestic market depends on preserving the exporting sectors' price competitiveness, and work is stable as long as there is sufficient mobilisation in favour of maintaining this competitiveness.
- A 'shortage and investment-oriented' mode translates periods of political and military and economic mobilisation, used either for building foundations for economic development, or else to prepare for war or to rebuild afterwards. The mode was found in totalitarian regimes and in countries that had to re-build after the Second World War. The automobile market is basically limited to commercial and military vehicles, and to cars destined for leaders and administrations.

Table 2.1   The principal growth models

Modes	National income		Market	Labour	Dynamics	Contradiction
	Distribution	Growth				
competitive and competed	- depends on local and category-specific balance of power and on financial opportunism	- variable depending on firms' domestic and external competitiveness	- balkanised - unstable - some categories are excluded	- flexible - organises itself on a professional basis	- drop in real prices - limited market due to uncertainty of income	- seeks to defend situation that has been acquired - speculative practices
competitive and consumer-oriented		- consumption-driven	- heterogeneous - variable	- flexible - organises itself into branch-wide labour unions	- broadening of market - stimulation of investment	- lack of a virtuous circle leading to mass consumption
competitive and price export-oriented		- driven by export of competitive standard products	- heterogeneous - unstable - some categories are excluded	- abundant - poorly organised	- rapid industrialisation	- domestic market is limited, lack of a virtuous circle
co-ordinated and consumer-oriented	- nationally co-ordinated, moderately hierarchised, geared to productivity	- consumption-driven	- mass-oriented - moderately hierarchised - foreseesable	- organised into unions - makes demands	- total population can access mass consumption	- needs to find new economies of scale once market is saturated

co-ordinated and specialised export-oriented	- nationally co-ordinated, moderately hierarchised, geared to export competitiveness	- driven by export of specialised goods or services	- mass-oriented - moderately hierarchised - significant top-of-the-range	- organised into unions - cooperative - stable	- total population can access mass consumption - high wages work in favour of quality products	- risk of getting boxed into one specialisation, likely to become obsolete
co-ordinated and price export-oriented		- driven by export of competitive mundane products	- mass-oriented - moderately hierarchised - foreseeable	- organised into unions - cooperative - stable	- total population can access mass consumption	- other countries' reactions - rise in wages and exchange rate
inegalitarian and rent-oriented	- structurally inegalitarian - vote-catching	- erratic, depends on world prices for raw goods and agricultural products	- categories of owners, executives and dependents - sudden contraction or expansion	- flexible - poorly organised - dependent	- enriched on a period-to-period basis	- industrialisation process runs into significant hurdles
shortage and investments-oriented	- relatively egalitarian for most of the population	- depends on savings rate	- very limited - administered - foreseeable	- mobilised	- ensures full employment, creates solid industrial bases	- cannot perpetuate itself indefinitely

Boyer, R., Freyssenet, M, GERPISA, 2001

- An 'inegalitarian and rent-oriented' mode is characterised by a type of growth that is driven by the export of raw materials or agricultural products, and by the distribution of the gains derived from the highly inegalitarian incomes which stem from the vote-catching system. National income is appropriated by a few minorities who redistribute it in part to other dependent social groups, according to practical and political necessities. Changes in world prices rhythm a national growth that does not have enough autonomy to fend for itself when faced with the shocks and uncertainties that come out of the international economy. For this reason, the domestic market either experiences periods of sudden frenzy or else of brutal collapse, all of which are accentuated by frequent modifications in the legal framework within which production activities are carried out.

Of course, modes of growth cannot explain everything about demand and work. However, they do determine two essential elements for choosing a profit strategy: volume and structure.

`Profit strategies´

Inasmuch as market and labour (much like the institutions that accompany them) vary according to the growth mode that is involved, firms cannot exploit all profit sources at the same time.

Six profit sources are directly related to the production of goods and services:
- economies of scales, with fixed costs being distributed across the widest possible volume so as to reduce unit costs,
- the diversity of the products offered, this being something that makes it possible to extend demand to solvent clienteles by satisfying their particular expectations,
- product quality, enabling a higher sales price or increased market share,
- commercially relevant innovation, thus guaranteeing a monopoly income for a variable period of time,
- productive flexibility, allowing for a rapid adjustment of costs to variations in demand,
- permanent reduction in costs, so that sufficient profit margins can be maintained whatever the circumstances.

Of course, all firms are aware of the existence of these six sources of profit. However, they cannot all be exploited or combined with the same ease. Indeed, for some of these sources to be exploited at all, certain very specific market and labour conditions may be necessary, situations that might only exist in particular growth modes. For example, there is no use relying upon economies of scale if the conditions that enable a mass consumption do not exist – this being a bitter experience that Henry Ford went through in Japan and in Europe during the interwar period. Certain profit sources also feature contradictory requirements that make it difficult to exploit them simultaneously and with the same level of intensity. As such, they cannot be combined. It is difficult for example to achieve economies of scale when offering as many specific models as there are types of clientele. It is also dangerous for a firm seeking to make room for itself amid profitable rivals to try to compete with them whilst exploiting the same profit sources as the ones they are using (Porter, 1985).

The profit combinations that are feasible and exploitable constitute what we can call firms' 'profit strategies'. Without purporting to have compiled a comprehensive list of past profit strategies and without predicting all of the strategies that will be invented in the future, we have nevertheless been able to identify at least six profit strategies that were actually implemented in the automobile sector during the 20th century. These strategies have been labelled in such a way as to stress the profit source(s) they emphasise: 'quality' strategy, 'diversity and flexibility' strategy, 'volume' strategy, 'volume and diversity' strategy, 'permanent reduction in costs' strategy, and 'innovation and flexibility' strategy (table 2.2). Firms are therefore differentiated first and foremost by their profit strategy, before potentially being further subdivided to reflect the means that are used to implement these strategies.

`Productive models´

Insofar as our main concern is to understand the conditions in which a firm can be profitable, the term 'productive' should be understood in its widest possible sense, i.e., as the production of value added. It thus encompasses not only the manufacturing of goods and services, but also the design, management, sourcing and sales functions.

Profit strategies cannot be implemented with just any means that are available. The resources that are used must fulfil each strategy's specific requirements; and they must be coherent with one another. For example, the 'volume and diversity' strategy necessitates multi-functional equipment and polyvalent employees, whereas the 'volume' strategy requires a totally different process, one that is based on standardised production and on workers who are specialised in one type of

Table 2.2   Profit strategies, pre-conditions and requirements

Profit strategy	Characteristics	Conditions of relevancy		Implementation requirements			Company governance compromise
		Market	Labour	Product policy	Productive organisation	Employment relationship	
Diversity and flexibility	- profit margins based on products that specifically respond to distinct types of demand - rapid adjustment of costs to variations in demand	- heterogeneous, even balkanised - from variable to unstable	- autonomous, flexible and mobile workforce	- models with few parts in common - targeting different customer categories - price that is most lucrative	- design new models rapidly and for lowest cost - production changed whenever necessary	- remuneration of competency and flexibility - incentives so work is carried out within competitive timeframe	- to be developed by shareholders seeking remuneration, employees and suppliers who ought to be flexible and efficient
Quality	- profit margins based on products socially considered to be top-of-the-range or luxury goods - commercial distribution is international from the beginning	- well-to-do and affluent clientele - international	- skilled, working under constraint of having to maintain specialisation on international markets of national production	- offering models that express the social and economic position of a well-to-do and affluent clientele	- guaranteeing quality of supplies, maintaining quality throughout production process - ability to sell prestige factor	- maintaining the rare competence that guarantees quality and prestige - emphasis on professionalism and on good work	- developed by owners concerned with the brand, by wage earning professionals and by suppliers responsible for quality
Volume	- economies of scale through production of increasing quantities of standard model	- homogeneous - rising - national, then international	- abundant, unskilled and unionised workforce	- offering a product that satisfies basic individual transport needs	- standardisation and fluidification of production	- get people to accept undifferentiated work and repetition of identical acts	- to be developed primarily by executives together with most employees

Volume and diversity	- Combination of economies of scale for non-visible elements and economies of scope for visible elements	- moderately hierarchised, with transition from one segment to another over product life - national then international	- polyvalent and unionised workforce	- offering superficially different models with shared platforms - excluding niche vehicles, at the very bottom and top-of-range	- control the complexification variety creates in all domains - avoid simultaneous overcapacities or undercapacities	- achieve polyvalency - offering of moderately hierarchised wages - guarantee career development opportunities	- mainly developed by managers together with growing number of engineers and technicians, and with labour unions
Innovation and flexibility	- Profit margins based on innovative models that are a response to new expectations - Innovation rent exploited through saturation of potential demand before it is copied - Losses limited through rapid reconversion in case of failure	- partially rejuvenated by the periodically emerging practical and symbolic expectations of new sections within the general population	- entrepreneurial and opportunistic employees	- offering when needed conceptually innovative models that correspond to the expectations of those durable new sections of the population	- generate ability to innovate in a commercially relevant manner - develop highly responsive organisation in all areas	- emphasis on innovation, expertise and responsiveness	- become financially autonomous so as to be able to assume the necessary risks - pact between executives, innovators and responsive employees
Permanent reduction in costs	- costs cut in all circumstances - Other profit sources are exploited as long as they do not undermine the costcutting - Makes it possible to avoid taking technical, social, commercial and financial risks	- moderately hierarchised - emphasis on price, reliability and raising level of basic equipment	- semi-skilled and unionised employees - operating under external competitiveness constraint	- strict volume, diversity and quality of product offer - avoid having to innovate conceptually	- avoid major variations in production - design a productive organisation that can be improved on a step-by-step basis	- get employees to accept cost-cutting as well as its effects on jobs and on work	- mainly developed by executives, employees and suppliers - ensure that this is politically acceptable in light of the stringent competitive capacities

Boyer, R., Freyssenet, M, GERPISA, 2002

workstation (see chapters 5 and 6). Still, the means that firms apply are in fact often the outcome of successive choices that in hindsight may turn out to have been contradictory. They can also cause tensions between a firm's players, and even create external constraints.

The conditions in which strategic means can become coherent with a range of choices

The creation of a modicum of coherency between the means being used and the 'profit strategy' being pursued cannot be achieved or perpetuated unless the main players in the firm agree on the strategy – and on the means themselves. For example, there can be no durable profits for a company pursuing an 'innovation and flexibility' strategy if its protagonists cannot find a form of productive flexibility that is acceptable to all. Moreover, no agreement can be reached unless it offers all players an opportunity to realise their varying medium and long-term personal objectives.

Thankfully, the requirements of a given profit strategy can be satisfied in several different manners. It is in no way written in stone that it is compulsory to adopt one specific set of means when a given profit strategy is to be implemented. For example, a permanent reduction in costs can be achieved by other means than the ones thought up by Taiïchi Ohno, acknowledged to be the father of the Toyota production system. Note that following the crisis of work that erupted at Toyota in the early 1990s, the company was forced to cease its efforts to get employees to assume responsibility for reductions in standard working times. Moreover, it was also obliged to adjust downwards its expectations of the contributions that employees were supposed to make to savings in materials and tools (see chapter 7). The innovative capacity of a firm pursuing an 'innovation and flexibility' strategy can be sustained by setting up a system that encourages the emergence of imaginative people within the company – or conversely through an external recruitment of designers who have proved themselves whilst working for competitors or in other sectors. From a strategic point of view, the choice between these two solutions is about the same. They diverge greatly, however, with respect to the productive model. Each has a different way of modifying the internal company governance compromise and of affecting the product policy and employment relationship (see chapter 8).

There are a number of reasons why a variety of means can be used to fulfil the requirements of one and the same strategy. First and foremost, the different growth modes not only provide varying frameworks for generating such profit strategies, but they also constitute a resource centre that allows for the strategies' implementation. Growth modes infer the existence of certain means. Moreover, through the laws, rules, institutions and practices that they have generated, growth modes provide arguments in favour of adopting a certain type of means. It remains that there are situations in which a firm's actors may choose others means, as the following chapters will demonstrate.

The three components of a productive model

Firms' socio-productive configurations present many different aspects, and at first glance it is not easy to detect which need to be examined. One solution to this problem is to focus on which measures are necessary for the implementation of a given profit strategy. This indicates which requirements are crucial.

The profit strategy analysis that will be conducted in the following chapters will demonstrate that the main elements can be combined into three prime components: 'product policy', 'productive organisation ' and 'employment relationship'.

Product policy refers to target markets and market segments; to the design and range of the products on offer; to sales volume objectives; to the models' diversity; and to quality, novelty and margins.

Productive organisation refers to the methods and means that are chosen to enact the product policy; to the extent to which activities have been integrated; to their spatial breakdown; to the organisation of design, outsourcing, manufacturing and commercialisation; to the techniques used; and to the management criteria.

The employment relationship refers to systems of employee recruitment; to employment; to classifications; to direct and indirect remuneration; to promotion; to scheduling; to possibilities of expression; and to employee representation.

Defining productive models in a way that allows them to be identified

A productive model materialises at the conclusion of a largely unintentional process during which coherency is created between the product policy, the productive organisation and the employment relationship, on one hand, and the profit strategy that is being pursued, on the other. This can only be achieved once two conditions have been fulfilled: the strategy must be relevant within the framework of the growth mode that governs the economic and political entity within which the firm is deploying its activity; and a durable company governance compromise must be set up between the firm's various actors (owners, executives, employees, labour unions and suppliers) concerning the means that are to be used so that the chosen strategy can be implemented in a coherent manner.

Inversely, those firms that do not successfully invent or adopt a productive model (that is, which do not become durably viable) are those where the profit strategy is no longer relevant; and/or where the company governance compromise has not made it possible to devise means that are coherent and acceptable to all of the main players; and/or where the profit strategy is of dubious value for at least one of them.

Whenever the terms and contents of the company governance compromise are modified, the productive model is transformed into a new model. However, the new compromise may well come to fruition without any coherent means being in place. The productive model then becomes an incoherent socio-productive configuration, undermining the foundations of the firm's profitability and therefore its longevity.

An appropriate profit strategy can just as easily not lend itself to any productive model whatsoever, as we will see in the chapter below on the 'quality' strategy that was put in place after the Second World War.

The models' plurality is therefore predicated first of all on a differentiation between growth modes; then on the selection of a profit strategy; and finally on the adoption or invention of means for implementing this strategy (means that are coherent and acceptable to the actors in the firm). It has been possible to identify at least six productive models in the automobile sector over the course of the 20th century: Taylor, Woollard, Ford, Sloan, Toyota, and Honda. Their characteristics, the profit strategy they pursue, the national modes of growth within which they can prosper, their history and their possible future are presented in the following chapters and summarised in table 9.1 at the end of the book. The process for engendering productive models can be summarised and represented by figure 2.1.

Definition of productive models

Productive models can be defined as 'company governance compromises' enabling a durable implementation of those profit strategies that are viable for the growth mode frameworks of the countries in which a firm is organising its activities, thanks to a series of means (product policy, productive organisation and employment relationship) that are coherent and acceptable to the people involved.

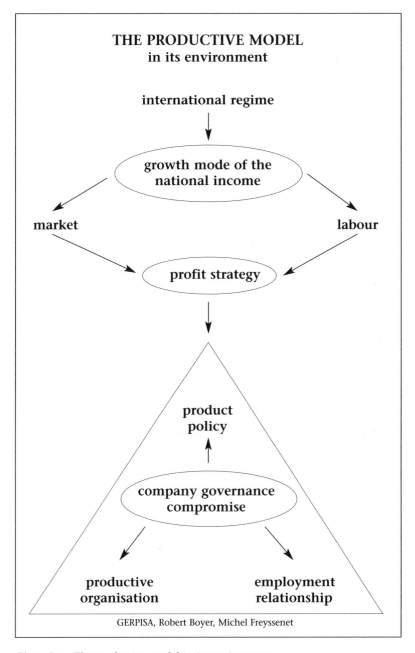

Figure 2.1 The productive model in its environment

What do we mean by a model?

In social sciences, a model is customarily referred to in four different ways. Each of these notions creates certain problems yet contains at least one aspect that should be taken into account when searching for a more operative concept.

An ideal to be attained

In the grand tradition of the Scientific Organisation of Work, a model is that system of production which guarantees the best results. There supposedly exists a one best way that firms must adopt if they do not want to be eliminated by their competitors. Yet there is no lack of examples of solutions that diverge but which have similar outcomes. Nevertheless, we should retain the idea that a model should be a socio-productive configuration that is likely to galvanise the actors in a firm so that they work to increase its performance.

A stylised set of attributes that really do exist

A model is a sort of small-scale map of socio-productive practices. Firms are grouped according to the number of attributes they share. Constellations of attributes that are correlated with one another and which feature positive financial results are deemed to be models. This conception raises a host of problems: it is very dependent on available data; it leads to a proliferation of different types; and it blurs divergences (differing meanings for one and the same attribute). Its aim should however be kept in mind – to ascertain those socio-productive configurations that actually do perform well, and not just those models that have been made popular by their inventors or by management sciences.

Building logical sequences based on players' allegedly fundamental behaviour

Here a model is seen as a method for detecting the coherency of a socio-productive configuration by means of a theoretical construct that supposedly reproduces the nub of the participants' behaviour. These theoretical constructs, notably those that have been developed by many economists, are unfortunately based far too often on abusive simplifications that have caused people to believe that such practices result from rational calculations which are intended to optimise outcomes. It is true that people must seek to ensure the longevity of the company for which they are working, i.e., its profitability. But there are many different ways to make profits – and to make losses.

A coherent response to the problems caused by previous developments

To understand the true meaning of these technical, organisational, managerial and social changes, they are analysed as if they are responses to the problems that are inherent to a dynamic itself, inherited either from an earlier stage of the division of labour, or else from the preceding productive model and corresponding institutional regime. It has become apparent that these changes should be analysed instead as attempts to cope with an uncertain outcome – and that they comprise one solution amongst a whole range of possibilities.

The productive model as a largely unintentional process that creates an external relevancy and internal coherency for the changes

The preceding critical examination has caused productive models to be thought of as a largely unintentional process for creating an external relevancy and internal coherency for these technical, organisational, managerial and social changes, in order that they may respond to the new problems of economic profitability and social acceptability that have been born out of the previous models' dynamics and out of transformations in the competitive, macroeconomic and societal contexts. An approach identifying this sort of model should be substantive (describing the contents of the practices), historical (identifying the problems faced so as to understand what the practices actually mean) and analytical (process of building the firm's profitability through the creation of a modicum of external relevancy and internal coherency for the changes). (Boyer, Freyssenet, 1995).

3
A `quality´ strategy that is still waiting for a productive model

Seen from the vantage point of the early 21st century, the work that was carried out in the first automobile factories was something akin to craftsmanship, in that it involved machinist manufacturing professionals and/or assemblers who sometimes had to adjust certain parts manually – and who were not subjected to the stringency of specified operational modes. In reality, after spending an initial two or three years finalising prototypes, the first car makers would usually start to organise their production industrially – having by this time applied a high level of division of labour.

There is a dearth of historical studies on the productive model(s) at work in the first half of the 20th century during this implementation of a 'quality' strategy – with all of the components thereof (notably wage-related and financial). However, it has been possible to establish that despite their repeated efforts, 'specialist' top-of-the-range manufacturers during the latter half of the century time and again found it difficult to build a productive model that could guarantee durable profitability.

A `craft production´ that is nowhere to be found

In France and in the United States particularly, very early on people were fully aware that production could be aligned into successive phases in order to reduce the number of handling operations. They also knew about the use of specialised machine tools to obtain interchangeable parts (Fridenson, 1982). Before getting into the car business, the sector's first protagonists had in general either been industrialists involved in a mass production of bicycles, fixed engines or carts; or else manufacturers of machine tools, plumbing articles and even automobile parts.

By 1900, the American automobile industry, even though it had only produced 3,000 petrol-powered automobiles, was already absorbing more than a quarter of the nation's total output of machine tools (Laux, 1982). Simplified manufacturing processes and interchangeable parts were on everybody's minds. Chassis stamping and cold pressing techniques replaced earlier cutting and forging methods, with wheels appearing from the beginning of the new century, first in Europe and then in the United States. Special steel also went through a number of changes, making it possible to diminish vehicle weight even as the reliability of parts and the precision of machining began to rise. Once production volumes had reached certain levels, car makers could begin to make use of specialised high-speed machines. Harry Leland, who founded Cadillac in 1902, had been trained in the interchangeability of parts whilst working for Colt, a gun manufacturer. At Brown and Sharpe he learned how to design specialised precision machine tools. When he finally got around to car making, his goal was to achieve a highly precise and standardised level of machining so that all parts on his models could be exchanged with one another on a standard basis.

In this so-called era of 'craft production', what we discover in fact are car makers who were pursuing at least two different types of profit strategy: a 'quality' strategy that is studied in the present chapter, and a 'diversity and flexibility' strategy that is analysed in the following one. These profit strategies were dominant for a long time, particularly in Europe and Japan where the demand for automobiles was too fragmented and limited for people to be able to rely on economies of scale. The 'quality' strategy remains one of the main profit strategies to be found in the automobile industry.

The `quality'-based profit strategy

This is the strategy that is being followed by today's so-called top-of-the-range and luxury car makers, long called 'specialist' manufacturers as opposed to 'generalist' manufacturers who target a wider market. Moreover, this was the strategy pursued by most car makers at the dawn of the automobile industry, when due to high production and utilisation costs cars could only be bought by well-to-do customers.

Other profit sources are subordinate to the product's `social quality'

Quality refers to the reliability and finishing of a product, the materials used, the number and type of accessories or styles, the level of perfection or mechanical innovation, the after-sales service and/or the symbolic signs of social distinction. The criteria vary over time, in space, and they differ by type of clientele. Quality is a source of profit when it is perceived by target customers as being superior to that which the competitors offer. It then allows a manufacturer to increase market share and/or to set prices that can vary depending on the circumstances.

A 'quality' strategy stresses those quality aspects that will make people see the product as being socially superior. Here profits basically originate from the margins that a top-of-the-range product and a well-off clientele can justify – the high price actually being a crucial mark of distinction and social exclusivity, above and beyond material justification. The product's symbolic branding is cultivated with great care.

In this strategy, the other sources of profit (volume, diversity, innovation, flexibility, cost reduction) play a secondary or even minor role. Quality is only socially distinctive if not everyone has access to it. As a result, volume cannot be exploited per se. Nor is any particular effort made to commonalise parts between the various models, as each model has to distinguish its own 'essential' nature from all the others', including and maybe even above all as regards its non-visible parts. The number of models is relatively high given the size of the top-of-the-range market, but it is of course smaller than the range that 'generalist' firms offer. On the other hand, there are a number of different versions, variants and options; and 'quality' can be extended all the way to include a product's level of customisation. Innovation is an important trait of social distinction. It is a sign of modernity that certain well-to-do social groups would like to convey, but it must be compatible with reliability, refinement, comfort and respectability (these being the prime markers of a top 'quality' product). All in all, this type of product innovates with its mechanical improvements and in terms of the comfort and safety of the equipment that it offers. It is not a conceptual innovation that relates to the product's actual usage and/or which responds to expectations emanating from new social categories. Productive flexibility, which according to the definition given in chapter 2 signifies an immediate adaptation of employment and investment to variations in demand, is not obligatory. Having lengthy delivery times whenever demand exceeds production possibilities contributes to the product's socially discriminating image. It is sometimes better to raise prices than to increase production capacities. Nor is a permanent reduction in costs a priority. Competition with other 'specialist' firms involves first and foremost the ability to embody the apex of a social hierarchy during a given era.

A top-of-the-range international market and a workforce renowned for its professionalism

To pursue a 'quality' strategy, there needs to be a well-to-do and privileged clientele which feels that it needs to use the automobile product to distinguish itself from society's other categories. This clientele can be observed in all known growth modes, but it is more or less extensive, separated from other market segments and fragmented and variable depending on the source of national income and on the way in which income is distributed. When distribution is 'co-ordinated and moderately hierarchised', the top-of-the-range is less cut off from the rest of the market, more homogeneous, larger in size and more stable, notably in those modes where growth is driven by the export of specialised goods (thus justifying higher salaries being paid to a greater number of people). Where distribution is competitive in nature, however, the top-of-the-range is clearly separated from the other market segments. It is fragmented and variable, particularly in the 'competitive and competed' and 'competitive and price export-oriented' modes. The top-of-the-range is divided into a myriad of sub-markets – and it would be commercially imprudent to confuse one of these segments with any of the others. In the 'inegalitarian and rent-oriented' mode it fluctuates to an even greater extent, following variations in world prices for raw materials and agricultural products, as well as speculative movements.

They are very few countries in which a small part of the population isn't ready to pay a high price to own products that symbolise its position at the top of the economic and social hierarchy. This is why the market for top-of-the-range products was (and has remained) an international one from the very outset.

A 'quality' strategy also infers the availability of a workforce that is for the most part highly skilled (and which is reputed as such). Certain aspects of quality can in fact only be obtained by using the services of traditional professional workers (or inversely, of technicians and even engineers who are graduates of the top universities) to manufacture parts in small series on highly sophisticated machinery. The reputation of a top-of-the-range brand is often related to the renown of its country of origin or of the region in which it is established, when this is famed for the personnel's seriousness and professionalism. In general, a 'quality' strategy is enhanced when the workforce is forced to maintain the national output's international specialisation, notably so as to be able to continue benefiting from the high salary levels, social protection systems and stable employment perspectives that are enabled by a production of specialised products that remain without rivals.

Regarding the market or labour, the 'co-ordinated and specialised export-oriented' growth mode is the one that affords the greatest via-bility to the 'quality' strategy. Competitive distribution modes do not stand in the way of this strategy. It allows many people to seek their for-tune, yet at the same time it is less stable. It relies on the availabil-ity of workers who are skilled but less attached to their firm.

Products that symbolise fortune and privilege; quality during all phases of the production process; enhanced professionalism

The means that must be found if a 'quality' strategy is to be pursued must first and foremost help to build, preserve and rejuvenate the top-of-the-range reputation of the car maker that has adopted this strategy.

The product policy must make it possible to offer products that not only express the superior social position of the buyer, but also the legit-imacy and respectability of his/her position. The car maker is a sort of social organiser for social categories that are comprised of property own-ers and/or business executives, and this for one of the most visible of all products. It might be that there is no need to revolutionise the product, but the manufacturer must nevertheless ensure that it is a leader in terms of performance, accessories, safety and reliability. The product can range from a luxury car that is more or less turned out on a one-by-one basis for extremely wealthy customers, to top-of-the-range cars pro-duced in medium series for well-paid upper middle class customers.

The productive organisation must first and foremost guarantee the product's 'social' quality. The number of vehicles that each employee turns out and the size of the stocks of parts are less important as factors than are the rate of defects or ensuring that the options being offered are those that the customer has actually requested. The work times allocat-ed to the various operations must allow each phase to achieve a level of 'finishing' that is difficult to formalise through standard operational rules. Quality control at each stage of the manufacturing process and the multitude of parts that can be used to customise the product bring about a production process that is discontinuous or fragmented. Suppliers must be known for the excellence of their output, and relationships with them have to be based on mutual trust between 'professionals'. The maker must always stress the fact that the methods being used differ from those that are applied in the production of mundane products.

The employment relationship must be such that it is possible to recruit a workforce that possesses the necessary level of skills. This workforce must also be encouraged (through career development and recognition of a job well done) to feel that it is a member of the firm and therefore a guarantor of its good name.

The proliferation, collapse, resurgence and transformation of the top-of-the-range manufacturers

Luxury car makers proliferated and prospered until the late 1920s, not only in Europe but also in the United States – even as America's large series manufacturers (Ford and General Motors, for example) were beginning to experience sudden expansion. The competitive distribution of incomes which prevailed at the time in these countries simultaneously encouraged a broadening of the upper classes (and therefore of the customer base for top-of-the-range products) and a rising standard of living for those independent and professional categories who, in a country as large as the United States, constituted a market that was sizeable enough for mass production to become viable. This was a time when top-of-the-range car makers were launching models which featured unprecedented levels of horsepower, cars that were refined but costly. This was the segment that was particularly affected by the Great Depression of 1929.

In the United States, the category of vehicles selling for more than $2,500 fell from 10 per cent of the total market during the 1920s to one per cent in the 1930s. It was not the competition from Ford, General Motors or even Chrysler that caused so many problems for top-of-the-range car makers – rather it was the collapse and shrinkage of their own specific market. In addition, they had to cope with a liquidity crisis that prevented them from retaining their teams of skilled workers, who were therefore no longer available to them once economic recovery had returned (Raff, 1998).

The change in growth modes after the Second World War was a second test for those manufacturers who had been pursuing a 'quality' strategy. The landscape of the top-of-the-range segment was changed by the fact that most industrialised countries adopted a 'co-ordinated and moderately hierarchised' type of national income distribution. The category's differentiation from the other market segments lessened as a result of the tightening of income inequalities. Volumes rose due to the increasing number of people earning high wages.

The generalist manufacturers were tempted to 'move upscale' inasmuch as it had become commercially possible to commonalise parts between top-of-the-range and upper mid-range models. For the first time, 'specialist' car makers were in direct competition with the 'generalists' – with the former group ultimately disappearing in the United States. In Europe, on the other hand, they soon learned how to adjust to the changing composition (and expectations) of the top-of-the-range clientele. Europeans were able to design vehicles that handled well, and which were powerful and comfortable. They also started to make 'sporty' cars that were quick and very attractive. And they were able to retain the necessarily skilled workforce.

Not only were certain luxury car makers able to resist the trend, but they even began to develop overseas, notably by penetrating the American market. They achieved this by turning their cars into global benchmarks for a new top-of-the-range category, and by emphasising quality, performance, mechanical perfection and innovative accessories.

The difficulties that the specialist car makers were facing stemmed in actual fact from their production system. The broadening of the demand for top-of-the-range products had caused them to adopt an assembly line organisation during the 1950s and 1960s, and to rely on an unskilled workforce for their assembly operations. The crisis of work that they experienced in the late 1960s specifically damaged the quality image that had been the foundation of their profitability.

Looking for a productive model: from assembly line to `reflexive production´ — and back again?

Volvo provides a good illustration of this point. Founded in 1927, the Swedish car maker was still producing fewer than 10,000 passenger cars per year in 1950. Until that point, it had been pursuing a 'diversity and flexibility' strategy, following the British example of offering a wide variety of models, and adopting a similar production system (see chapter 4). However, Sweden then moved to a growth mode that was based on the export of specialised goods and on an income distribution mode that featured a minimum of hierarchisation. In addition, the country's borders were opened, and its standard of living generally rose – all of which caused Volvo to specialise in the top-of-the-range segment. The company reduced the number of models that it offered to two cars that were designed to be robust, durable and safe, targeting an international clientele of relatively well-to-do families with three children or more and who were living in a basically (sub)urban environment.

A crisis of work that affected `quality' production in a full employment environment

After an early but short-lived attempt (due to a widespread labour strike in 1952) to introduce an assembly line and a time and motion method (TMM), Volvo finally pushed this initiative through in 1964 with its opening of a complete assembly plant and engine factory at Gothenburg (Glimsted, 2000). However, given that this took place in an environment of full employment, the firm soon had to cope with a rise in absenteeism, an increase in worker resignation rates and a drop in product quality. German specialist car makers experienced similar problems at about the same time.

Volvo tried to devise 'socio-technical' solutions to this work crisis by significantly extending the duration of the production cycle, introducing modular work and systematically improving the workstations' ergonomics. Its quality image, essential for commercial survival, was reinforced by an advertising campaign that focused on the new production methods and on how they differed from 'mass production'.

From the `enriching of work' to `reflexive production'

In 1974, Volvo opened its Kalmar plant, which has since become a symbol of the so-called 'socio-technical' path. The plant was organised into workshops, each of which corresponded to a vehicle component. In each workshop automated guided vehicles were circulated upon which workers assembled the relevant components by picking the necessary parts out of boxes that were arranged alongside the vehicle circuit. The work cycle time was extended (sometimes reaching 15 minutes) and the operational variety significantly increased. The work cycle time corresponded to the amount of time that each worker needed to carry out a series of operations on a product that was advancing at a fixed speed along the manufacturing line, before having to repeat the same operations (Sandberg, 1995).

This system was meant to enable a production of high quality goods at an acceptable cost both in a product renewal market and in an environment marked by a shortage of labour. The absenteeism reduction target was achieved, but worker resignation rates remained too high, and worst of all workers at Kalmar did not have the feeling that the announced revolution in work content was actually happening. In reality, the operational sequencing and distribution of tasks amongst workers remained determined by the need to 'saturate' the work cycle time via a centralised and programmed control of the automated guided vehicles rather than by a product building logic that would render the work intelligible and give it renewed meaningfulness.

The sharp recovery in Sweden's (and specifically in Volvo's) exports after 1982 led to a new shortage in labour even as unemployment was exploding across Europe. Volvo was again forced to increase the attraction of working in one of its factories. In 1985 it decided to 'go even further' than it had done at Kalmar with the new assembly plant it built at Uddevalla.

Breaking completely not only with assembly line principles but also with the concept of dividing a manufacturing line into a succession of phases, Uddevalla was entirely given over to a method wherein vehicles were completely assembled by two or three workers operating out of stationary workstations. This became possible because of two innovations: parts and small components were automatically brought in from a central warehouse on automated guided vehicles; and they were stacked on shelves according to their location and function in the car. The memorisation of logically unrelated assembly line operations, a source both of numerous errors in the past and of a general lack of interest in the work being done, was replaced at Uddevalla by an understanding of the product's inherent production logic and by the utilisation of people's ordinary cognitive capabilities. Experience showed that by so doing it is possible to save time in comparison with standard assembly line methods (Ellegard, Engström, Nilsson, 1991: Nilsson, 1995).

As such, 'reflexive production' did away with the time wastage that the mechanised assembly lines had generated structurally. With the latter, it was impossible to saturate the work cycle time, and tasks had to be reshuffled each and every time there was a change in production or a variation in demand. The whole process had to be shut down if there was an incident or a breakdown at any point along the line, and the firm had to keep replacement personnel on hand in case anyone was absent, etc. (see chapter 5). 'Reflexive production' also enables an adjustment of output to demand by simplifying assembly workstation shutdowns or start-ups. This means that product variety can be increased without output being disturbed. Assemblers are provided with an overview, and they can control the vehicle's general quality – something that is not possible with assembly line work. Lastly, the new system allows for much greater product diversity (and even customisation) without any lengthening in total assembly time (Freyssenet, 1998a).

The principles of 'reflexive production' cannot be implemented profitably unless employees work within the time limits that are allocated to them, participate in the reduction of standard times and take part in product improvement processes. In and of itself, carrying out an intelligent and skilful type of work does not mean that employees will be participating in the continual rise in performance. In addition, there remains some residual risk that employees will cash in their new competencies elsewhere, or that their absences will become more frequent without it becoming any easier to replace them. As such, if this type of production system is going to become a productive model, it still needs to find an employment relationship that is coherent, and which is acceptable for all of the firm's players.

During the 1990s, to regain its competitiveness Sweden was forced to get rid of a number of social benefits, and to use unemployment as a tool of policy. It is in no way certain that this country will in the future be able to provide a framework in which a productive model that is based on the principles of 'reflexive production' can be developed. Nor is it certain that Volvo, ever since it was sold to Ford, can become the inventor of such a model.

The future of the 'quality' strategy

The 1990s were characterised by a sea change in the general environment. With income distribution having become more 'competitive', the top-of-the-range segment tended to become more heterogeneous. Demand for very top-of-the-range saloon cars (which had become marginal products) rose again. Above all, 'top-of-the-range' demand cropped up for small and medium-sized cars and for recreational vehicles.

These developments have presented the 'specialist' manufacturers with a new situation. On one hand, if they are to cover the new top-of-the-range sub-segments they must make substantial increases in their design-related spending, productive capacities and distribution network. On the other, they must fight off ambitious 'generalists' who also want to benefit from the new situation. To cope, they have adopted a variety of different paths.

Saab, Aston Martin, Jaguar and Volvo have ultimately opted to be integrated into a large automobile group – General Motors for the former, Ford the others. By so doing, they hope to avail themselves of the resources they need. However, the logic of the 'volume and diversity' strategy that General Motors has been pursuing (see chapter 6) entails a further commonalisation of the platforms upon which GM's marques build their models, even if this means taking a risk that the top-of-the-range cars will lose their essential 'quality', i.e., their specificity. This seems to be the dilemma that Ford has been facing with its top-of-the-range marques. Fiat, which was forced to take over Lancia in the 1970s and Alfa Romeo in the 1980s, made these marques lose a large part of their prestige when it decided to launch, in their name, models whose platforms were actually being shared with Fiat's own models.

A second path for which a number firms have opted is that of external growth. This involves acquiring other car makers who already cover, or else who are likely to cover, the new sub-markets of the top-of-the-range category. This was BMW's path when it purchased Rover in 1994 and Rolls-Royce in 1999. Rolls-Royce's new models have yet to come out. Land Rover's recreational vehicles were already positioned at the top-of-the-range. With a few design modifications and a handful of vigorous actions aimed at improving manufacturing quality, Rover's small and medium-sized cars could have been integrated into a product range for well-to-do customers. However, for this to succeed, the policy would have had to have been carried out energetically and without wasting time, especially since the continued rise in the value of the British Pound was cutting the company off from a significant chunk of its potential export market. To avoid a catastrophe, BMW had to sell Rover in 2000 to an English consortium for a token sum. On the other hand, it was able to sell Land Rover to Ford at a good price. All that BMW has retained from this adventure is the world-famous Mini, which it has turned into a small top-of-the-range urban vehicle. Weakened by these events, BMW itself has even become a takeover target for other car makers (although up until now it has succeeded in remaining independent).

Daimler (Mercedes) has chosen yet another path. In truth, its trajectory is relatively opaque and may even turn out to be full of danger. In successively acquiring Chrysler and Mitsubishi and in taking a stake in Hyundaï, Daimler has been embarking on two possible trajectories. Either it can become an automobile giant, turning out all kinds of vehicles for all sorts of clients, or else it can remain a top-of-the-range car maker but for all types of vehicles. The difficulty is that neither Chrysler nor Mitsubishi are 'generalist' manufacturers, even though they have regularly tried to achieve this status. Nor are they top-of-the-range car makers. The only times that either have made a profit is when they have reverted to their original strategy, that is, to a strategy based on 'innovation and flexibility'. Yet the requirements of this strategy are such that it is almost totally incompatible with any other (see chapter 8).

Industrial history is full of paradoxes. The paradox that we are focusing on at present is that the main 'specialist' car makers have been either losing their independence; or else thinking that they must change their strategy at the very moment that the international market for top-of-the-range products is most likely to launch them on a new phase of expansion.

4

The `diversity and flexibility´ strategy and the Taylor and Woollard models

The 'diversity and flexibility' strategy was the second profit strategy to have been pursued by car makers who have been inaccurately described as 'craft' manufacturers. It was relevant until the Second World War, in Europe as well as in Japan and the United States. Many American car makers pursued this strategy until the Great Depression, and many European car makers did the same until the 1940s (wich British firms perpetuated until the 1960s, that is, until the formation of British Leyland). Some were able to achieve a profitable implementation of this strategy by adopting a Taylor model – with others having invented a Woollard model.

The necessary conditions if this sort of strategy is to be viable had disappeared from the aforementioned countries or regions (except Great Britain) by the second half of the 20th century. However, they could easily return if a 'competitive' distribution of income were to establish itself for the long haul, 'balkanising' demand again as was the case during the first half of the century.

The `diversity and flexibility´ profit strategy

A diverse product offer can be a source of profit insofar as it broadens demand by responding to each customer category in a relevant manner, i.e., reflecting that category's financial resources, practical needs, tastes and symbolic expectations. Diversity can involve all of a vehicle, or just part of it. It therefore ranges from an offering which features models that are entirely distinct in nature to simple variations relating to little more than the vehicle's accessories, body or internal fittings.

Productive flexibility is also a source of profit when it enables companies to adjust costs more rapidly than their competitors do to variations in demand, both at a quantitative and at a qualitative level. This can range from simple quantitative adjustments to the ability to rapidly convert to a product that can better satisfy the expectations of all or part of the targeted customer base.

Diverse specific products and a flexibility that depends on variations in demand

The 'diversity and flexibility' strategy entails offering as many specific models as there are economically and socially distinct clienteles; producing only those products for which orders exist; and adopting costs continually. The other profit sources only manifest themselves on the odd occasion.

Economies of scale are limited by the fact that the production runs are at best small or medium-sized; and by the way in which fixed costs are brought down as part of the desire to facilitate productive flexibility. Quality is secondary to the imperative that a specific and distinctive product be supplied. Innovation is only important when it is necessary to improve the relevancy of the response being provided to the expectations of a particular type of clientele. Nor is the permanent reduction of costs a priority, since instead of being price-based, competition relates to the product's suitability.

A heterogeneous market and a flexible workforce

This strategy is only appropriate where the market is heterogeneous and the work flexible. A heterogeneous market is one in which demand is not structured as a continuum from the bottom to the top-of-the-range, rather where it is broken down into distinct compartments, each of which has its own requirements. Here flexible work is one whose duration and volumes continually mirror market demand.

This is how things worked in the 'competitive and consumer-oriented' mode – and to an even greater extent in the 'competitive and competed' one. In the latter mode, growth varies to reflect firms' competitiveness, with income distribution depending both on the balance of power at the local and professional levels and also on financial opportunism. Social relationships are so fraught that each category seeks above all to defend its own position (hence a series of inwardly-focused behaviours and the advent of identity politics). Mirroring this situation, the automobile market tends to become unstable and 'balkanised': unstable because the various social and professional categories' incomes are never durably guaranteed; and 'balkanised' because each category expects the purchased object to be a mark of its specificity and a sign of its cohesion. As for labour, it can be flexible yet at the same time also be organised on a category-specific basis: flexible because inter-firm mobility is frequent, with people trying to maximise their pay wherever the labour market allows for this (given the uncertain future); and organised by category because in anticipation of less favourable times, professional groups try to obtain or defend (each independently of the other) their autonomy and the advantages they have acquired.

Specific products, flexible organisation and an incentivising employment relationship

The means that have to be found if a 'diversity and flexibility' strategy is to be implemented must enable firms to offer specific products in the right quantity and at a remunerative price.

Products must be clearly imputable (in terms of their attributes) to their target market. For this reason, they can share no more than a few parts at the very most.

The productive organisation must be such that products can be designed rapidly and inexpensively. It must enable the manufacturing process to be changed as often as is needed to track variations in the demand for the different models. The design teams should be small, and they should work closely together with the manufacturing people to ensure that the models are launched rapidly and at a low cost.

Manufacturing and assembly operations should not necessitate any heavy fixed outlays on materials, since this would reduce the feasibility of rapid adjustments and ultimately increase costs. Tooling changes whenever there is a shift from one production run to another must be as rapid and inexpensive as possible. Workshop supply systems must avoid time-wasting, and should not allow much intermediary stock to accumulate. As such, flexibility is basically a reflection of what the personnel actually does.

Lastly, the employment relationship must compensate for this flexibility, yet at the same time it must also create a framework in which a given quantity of work can be carried out within a competitive period of time.

Historically, at least two models have fulfilled the requirements of the 'diversity and flexibility' strategy: the Taylor and Woollard models. They differ in terms of their 'company governance compromises' and their means of implementation.

The Taylor model was not originally designed for mass production

Our presenting the Taylor model as a system that makes it possible to pursue a diversity and flexibility-based profit strategy may be surprising to the reader, seeing as this model has become synonymous with uniformity and rigidity. As such, we should first review what it was that Taylor was actually trying to achieve.

In reality, what Taylor had envisaged was a complete production system whose purpose would be to resolve the typical manufacturing problems of small or medium-sized production runs, whether this involved stationary workstation assembly or a non-mechanised line. Such problems stemmed from what Taylor called workers' 'soldiering', i.e. workers' deliberate attempts to slow down their work pace. He believed that this was mainly the consequence of employers' practice of lowering per unit pay rates and reducing staffing levels once increases in hourly output had somehow been obtained (Taylor, 1902, 1911). Of course, Taylor was gone by the time that work paces had begun to be imposed upon workers by machines or by mechanised assembly lines.

Now, according to Taylor, an enormous output gap existed between a very good worker and an average one (the former producing two to four times as much as the latter). In Taylor's words, a very good worker can sustain efforts 'without injury to his health ... throughout a working lifetime'. Furthermore (and using a provocative turn of phrase), Taylor also stated that it was possible to reconcile higher wage levels and a cheaper workforce by focusing on increasing the amount of value-added rather than on discussions of profit-sharing. Workers' and employers' interests could be reconciled if the former were prepared to work to the maximum of their personal abilities and physical aptitudes, and if the latter paid them '30 to 100% per cent more than the average for workers in their category.' Based on his own experience, Taylor felt that workers would go along with this regime if there were an impartial determination of the most efficient sequencing of their operations (and of their work times) – as stated in the 'scientific method' that he was preaching. Towards this end, a specialised department, managed by an engineer working together with the most experienced and best performing employees, should be created to analyse and to time tasks, whether or not they involved skilled operations.

The establishment of a standard operational sequence did not undermine the underlying intellectual logic of tasks. This would occur at a

The changing meaning of the expression `Taylorism´

The term 'Taylorism', which first arrived in France in the 1920s as a name for the 'Scientific Organisation of Work' method that was thought up by Frederick Winslow Taylor in his seminal book *Shop Management* (1902), grew in importance as it was being diffused. By the 1970s it had become synonymous with a separation between the design and execution of work – a division whose epitome was supposed to be the parcellisation of tasks (a type of organisation that many attributed to Taylor).

Taylorism's growing fame and the concomitant change in the meaning of this term resulted from a conjunction of many different factors. Purporting to be a way of reconciling employers' and employees' interests through the use of undisputed scientific studies of work, Taylorism benefited from the rapid rise in the fortunes of workplace engineers, a category where it found enthusiastic propagandists, notably in France (Moutet, 1992). It was also very attractive to left-wing labour unions and political movements, Lenin himself having requested its application in an effort to accelerate workers' training and to introduce indispensable discipline to the workplace (Linhart, 1976).

In the aftermath of the Great Depression, Taylorism became the target of a double criticism. On one hand, it was seen to be overly managerial because it neglected the significance of 'human relationships' in the workplace (Mayo, 1933). On the other, it was criticised for the de-humanisation of work – a trend for which it was ultimately held responsible (Friedmann, 1936). As such, the meaning of the expression 'Taylorism' was considerably extended, not only becoming assimilated with the Ford system but also, and to an even greater degree, with concepts such as industrial rationalisation and even industrial civilisation. The modernist euphoria of the postwar period, an era when many people were convinced that automation would make it possible to transcend the parcellisation of work (Touraine, 1955), softened these criticisms to a certain extent. But the debate was spectacularly revived by the work and productivity crises of the late 1960s.

Certain sociologists, reassessing and deepening the division of labour analyses that Marx had carried out a century earlier, saw Taylorism as one of the forms of the 'division of the intelligence of labour' process that crops up at a given moment in the history of the relationship between capital and labour (Braverman, 1974; Freyssenet, 1974). Various leaders and managers accused Taylorism of being a cause for employees' growing loss of interest in their work and the source of many firms' difficulties in satisfying a demand that was becoming increasingly diversified. On the other hand, other phenomena at least had the merit of convincing analysts that alternative paths were possible: a number of socio-technical experiments were carried out; variations were noticed in the extent of different countries', firms' and factories' division of labour; and 'Toyotaism' was discovered, a system that was thought to be capable of filling the gap between design and execution. The diffusion of microelectronics and of flexible automation, plus the requirements of an increasingly competitive and diversified market, lead certain parties to predict the arrival of a mode of production that would reconcile mass and customised production, industrial output and employees' personal fulfilment. It was at this time that people began to announce the advent of 'post-Taylorism'.

Nevertheless, many observers consider that Taylorism is synonymous with a separation between design and execution; and with an parcellisation of work. Yet Taylorism, as a historical specificity, does not entail a division between design and execution, something that began a century and a half earlier, and which later developed in many different forms. Nor does it involved an parcellisation of work, this having been the consequence of a production line organisation that only appeared at a later stage (Freyssenet, 1984).

later date, once production line work had begun to split operations up amongst different workstations solely so as to be able to 'saturate' the work cycle time for each of these positions (see chapter 5). The 'Taylor method' became a Taylor model when it was adopted by firms pursuing a 'diversity and flexibility' strategy – and when such firms adopted the method so as to become socially acceptable.

The Taylor model is a response to the demands of a 'diversity and flexibility' strategy, in that it allows for the production of medium-sized series of varied goods at competitive prices, thanks to tasks (skilled or other) that are organised into their design, manufacturing and administrative functions – the basis for this organisation being the procedures and operative rules that have to be followed, and the time allocations that the interested parties have defined together with a specialised department. The employment relationship is basically characterised by task-related wages that are augmented by 30 to 100 per cent – as long as procedures are respected and deadlines met.

This 'compromise' provided executives with greater productivity and flexibility; it gave more power to organisational engineers; and it offered higher individual wages to those employees who accepted the new working norms.

The Taylor model could only be profitably adopted as long as production runs were long enough to economically justify the preparation of tasks. It remains that this was the situation in which a number of American, Italian and French car makers found themselves during the interwar period (Nelson, 1975; Fridenson, 1972, 1977; Moutet, 1992; Bigazzi, 2000).

The Taylor model

The Taylor model is a productive model:

1. That implements a 'diversity and flexibility' profit strategy which is particularly relevant when the market is heterogeneous and when work is flexible, i.e. in the 'competitive and competed' and 'competitive and consumer-oriented' growth modes.

2. That fulfils the requirements of this strategy through:

 – a product policy that offers models which are specific, varied, produced in medium-sized series and correspond to a demand that is economically and socially compartmentalised;

 – a productive organisation involving a pre-determination of the tasks that are to be accomplished (whether or not they are skilled) in the manufacturing, design and administrative functions. This consists of establishing procedures and operational rules that must be followed plus time allocations that must be respected (both being defined by all interested parties together with a specialised department);

 – an employment relationship in which wages are markedly higher than elsewhere – as long as procedures are followed and deadlines met.

3. Thanks to a company governance compromise between executives, organisational engineers and employees. The former benefit from the increased productivity, the second play an arbitrator's role and the latter receive higher individual wages.

The Woollard model

During the interwar period, British car makers knew all about specialised American machine tools, the Taylor method and the Ford production system. Nevertheless, they were forced to devise an original productive model in order to implement the 'diversity and flexibility' strategy that in their opinion was the only appropriate one for the English context of the time.

This original productive model can be called 'Woollard' since its father is thought to be Frank Woollard, an engineer who was manufacturing director at Morris (Boyer, Freyssent, to be published). Together with colleagues working for other British car makers, Woollard purposefully tried to create a model that was more relevant and which therefore performed better than the Ford system. His motivation was that his local market was a diversified and limited one – with workers who were hostile to any reduction in their autonomy and competency (Woollard, 1924, 1954).

In Woollard's vision, productive diversity and flexibility could be profitably combined with competent and autonomous employees if work were organised into stationary workstations or into short run manufacturing and assembly lines – as long as ways were found to keep inventory levels down; to limit the number of handling operations this organisation causes; and to get workers to work at a high enough pace.

The Woollard innovation consisted of the mechanisation and synchronisation, not of the product flow, but of the parts that were being shipped downstream towards the working zones. It also entailed setting up a piecework pay system replete with individual or group bonuses.

A synchronised and mechanised flow of parts; autonomous work teams

During the 1930s, the Morris plant at Cowley near Oxford had systematically applied the earlier principles. It was equipped with a 12-mile long aerial conveyor belt network (with around 10 branches and switches) so that any of the parts used in the plant's five different types of chassis and 15 body variants could be taken out of storage as they were needed. The network was also able to send the empty trolleys and carts back to the storage facilities. The work zones' supply operations were initiated by the work teams themselves. One of the members telephoned the storage facilities a half-hour in advance to request the necessary parts. As such, the process was steered by its downstream section. Sourcing flows were synchronised thanks to 'intermediary stock conveyors' with carefully calculated dimensions (Tolliday, 1998a). Productivity gains were achieved by getting rid of as many handling operations and worker movements as possible, and by 'fluidifying' the work zones' supply operations.

The manufacturing workers might have been able to preserve a modicum of autonomy, but this does not mean that they were 'skilled'. Skilled workers were gradually replaced by 'semi-skilled' ones. The machine tools that had been installed in the machining department were equipped with a limited number of 'universal' cutting tools and with templates designed by the tooling workshop – which gave specific dimensions for each type of parts. The same applied in the assembly area. Almost all of the parts being assembled were interchangeable, thanks to the earlier system – and assembly workers' adjustment operations, although they had not entirely disappeared, were limited to just a few actions (for which workers also received specific templates). However, on its own this system was neither capable of respecting the output targets it had been set, nor could it resolve the co-ordination problems that began to appear.

An incentive wage negotiated on a team-by-team basis

To achieve the target volumes and indispensable level of co-ordination, a special wage structure was set up. Called an 'incentive ' or 'inductive' system, this entailed paying wages on a piecework basis for a minimum production volume, with a very significant individual or group bonus being paid for anything beyond this threshold. The bonus could reach 50 to 100 per cent of basic wages. At Austin, parts were converted into fixed rate time units (Lewchuk, 1989, Tolliday, Zeitlin, 1991). Labour-management bargaining thus covered the number of time units need-ed to make each type of part (if workers were operating at a normal work pace) – and no longer piece work rates that were always subject to a great deal of debate. Work was therefore organised by work teams that were represented (and de facto captained) by union representatives. Shop stewards, members of the union for that particular category of work, negotiated piecework rates with the foremen and factory man-agers, in a sense becoming the guarantors of the production targets. Each team was responsible for running one segment of the production process.

Quantitative and qualitative flexibility

The first element of note in this system is that it entailed hardly any productive integration at all. Car manufacturers received supplies from a components making industry that was more concentrated than the automobile industry itself. In terms of their own workforce, car makers frequently shortened or extended the work day, hiring and firing to match variations in demand (regardless of whether these were season-al or cyclical in nature). The factors that made it possible to apply these practices were the competitive type of national labour relationship and the wage system that had been set up.

The production system was very flexible, at least whenever it was necessary to change the type of production (with two weeks sufficing sometimes for the changeover). The factories were not specialised on any particular model. There was a great deal of multi-skilling within the teams. On the other hand, the borders between the various workforce categories, such as they had been defined in collective agreements and defended by the individual unions, were hermetic.

English employers thought that the system was a very advantageous one. It enabled drastic reductions in the number of foremen, limited the need for pre-studies and for stringent norms, satisfied workers' demands for greater autonomy whilst motivating them to resolve by themselves their small sourcing and machine maintenance problems (in order to exceed their minimum volume targets) and created a zone of congruent interests between employers and employees.

The `diversity and flexibility' strategy loses its relevancy — and the crisis of the Taylor and Woollard models

American firms who had been pursuing a 'diversity and flexibility' strategy, especially those who had adopted the Taylor model, suffered

---

The Woollard model

The Woollard model is a productive model:

1. That implements a 'diversity and flexibility' profit strategy which is particularly relevant when the market is 'balkanised' and when work is flexible and organised on a professional basis, as is the case in a 'competitive and competed' growth mode.

2. That fulfils the requirements of this strategy through:

– a product policy that consists of offering specific models which are manufactured in small and medium-sized series, responding to a demand which emanates from customer bases that are clearly distinct at an economic and a social level;

– a flexible productive organisation which is steered backwards from downstream; emphasises mechanised and synchronised sourcing; and offers manufacturing and assembly workers (who are organised into work teams) the autonomy and know-how they need to make or assemble varied and variable products in small and medium-sized series;

– an employment relationship that is based on a system of hiring and scheduling that enables an adjustment of staffing levels and working durations to variations in demand and on an 'incentive' piecework pay system, where wages are augmented by a large personal or team bonus, inducing workers to organise themselves to reach target production volumes and to resolve those co-ordination problems that could keep them from succeeding in this endeavour.

3. Thanks to a company governance compromise between owners, executives and the different employee categories, wherein the former are guaranteed a constant return on their capital invested, the second benefit from the quantitative and qualitative flexibility they need to cope with a multi-faceted and variable demand without there being any pre-determination of the work organisation, and the latter enjoy work autonomy as well as a level of skills that allows them to negotiate piecework rates.

greatly from the Depression and from its aftermath. Whereas there had been 61 firms in this category in 1917 (their numbers had doubled in a decade, matching Ford's expansion), only 10 were still in business in the late 1930s. Their sales, which had been increased by a factor of six (reaching 1 million units), fell to 350,000 before the Second World War. A significant proportion of these car makers' customers had experienced a catastrophic drop in income. The establishment of a co-ordinated and moderately hierarchised income distribution mode from the 1940s onwards changed the nature of this demand, and rendered a 'diversity and flexibility' strategy inoperative.

In Great Britain, the Woollard model did survive the Second World War. Frank Woollard and his colleagues joined up again at British Motor Company after the 1952 merger between Austin and Morris. They developed automated systems for the machining and assembly work that was being carried out by teams of semi-skilled workers who, in line with the principles of the Woollard model, were still being paid a piecework rate plus bonus (Tolliday, 1998a; Zeitlin, 1999). BMC devised a type of machine head transfer equipment that was much more flexible than anything being used in the United States or in France at the time. This was a type of equipment in which interchangeable and reusable machine heads enabled the machining of all three types of engines that the firm's product range included. Rapid tool changes could be organised and carried out by specialised teams. The new Austin factory that opened in 1951 was equipped with automatic handling units allowing for the parallel assembly of three car models that came in several different versions. The 'intermediary stock conveyors' of the 1930s were replaced by smaller quantities of supplies that were mainly sourced from outside suppliers.

The Woollard model experienced a series of problems during the 1960s – hurdles that British car makers were unable to overcome. The 'diversity and flexibility' profit strategy they had been applying lost its relevancy as a result of various British governments' attempts to link income distribution to productivity gains (as was the case in most other industrialised countries) rather than to the balance of power at a local and professional level. The demand for automobiles became less balkanised. Ford's, Vauxhall's and the generalist European car makers' products became commercially more relevant and began to compete with the British firms' offerings. With their wages and very jobs under threat, workers tried to get some leverage from the power they held over the production process (and from their professional organisations). In addition, the productive organisation lost some of its flexibility, due to the increased integration of the production process.

During the 1970s, the various firms that had gradually constituted British Leyland tried to shift from a Woollard model to a Taylor one. They were hoping that this would lead to greater employee discipline at work. However, by this time the latter model had become just as unsuited to the new environment as the former one was (Church, 1994; Foreman-Peck J. et al., 1995; Mair, 1998)

A possible resurgence of the `diversity and flexibility´ strategy

Is the 'diversity and flexibility' strategy gone forever? Several countries have recently reverted to a competitive distribution of incomes and the social 'balkanisation' that they are beginning to manifest could well mean that this strategy will regain its relevancy. For the time being, this trend has strengthened the 'innovation and flexibility' strategy that is being pursued by Chrysler, Renault and Honda (see chapter 8). Yet if social relationships were to become more fraught and social categories less fluid, a 'diversity and flexibility' strategy could once again be imbued with relevancy. This may well be an opportunity for new 'entrants', i.e., firms who could benefit from the fact that the components making industry has become highly concentrated, hierarchised and internationalised (Lung, et al., 1998).

5
The 'volume' strategy and the Ford model

Henry Ford was the first car maker to totally commit to a 'volume' strategy that had long been applied in other industrial sectors. In late 1908, he designed and launched a single standardised car model, the Ford Model T. Production line work was introduced in 1913 and generalised in 1915. This involved a massive recruitment of unskilled labourers to whom Ford offered, from 1914 onwards, a fixed daily wage of $5 – twice as much as average workers were earning at the time. By 1927, worldwide output of the Ford Model T had reached 15,458,781 units. The peak annual output was reached in 1923 (2,055,309 units, including 1,414,293 in the United States). The economies of scale that were achieved enabled a lowering of the Model T's price from $850 when it was first launched to $360 in 1917. Henry Ford himself took responsibility for explaining his philosophy and production system in two books that were to enjoy a great deal of fame: *My Life and Work* (1922) and *Today and Tomorrow* (1926). More than anything else, he used this as an opportunity to develop the idea that it was necessary to regularly increase wages so as to constantly widen demand – this being a precondition for a truly mass type of industrial production.

From Ford to Fordism — and back again

Ford's spectacular performances, just like the radical newness of his production system and wage policies, captured the public's imagination. Not only were industrials enthusiastic, but right-wing and left-wing politicians, intellectuals, artists, union representatives, etc. were as well. A capitalist enterprise seemed capable of offering high wages and of lowering prices on luxury goods, thus rendering them accessible to an ever-greater proportion of the population – as long as people accepted the 'rationalisation' of work and the transformation of their lifestyles. Industrials preferred speaking of the 'Ford system' or 'Fordisation', with others in the 1930s even beginning to discuss a transformation of capitalism itself (following the example of Antonio Gramsci, a philosopher and co-founder of the Italian Communist Party). The French Regulation School rekindled this terminology during the 1970s to describe the process that had been observed during the post-war boom years, to wit, the redistribution of mass production-driven productivity gains via a generalised rise in the purchasing power of wages (Aglietta, 1976; Boyer, Mistral, 1978).

As fertile and necessary as these successive semantic extrapolations have turned out to be, it remains that they have partially masked the history of the Ford Motor Company, as well as the difficulties that it and its production system have had to face. They gloss over the basic differences between the Ford, Taylor and Sloan models. It therefore behoves us to take another look at the Ford production system, and at the crisis thereof, in order to understand why the Ford model did not really appear until after the Second World War – and why in fact only two car makers (Ford and Volkswagen) really adopted it.

The gradual and tentative shaping of the Ford production system

The son of an immigrant Irish farmer who had reached a certain level of prosperity, Henry Ford understood from very early on the considerable potential automobile market that farmers and independent professionals formed in a country as large as the United States – as long as these target groups were offered a product that satisfied their basic needs at a price that was accessible. He designed the Ford Model T to be large enough for a family yet usable by a single person. He made sure that it was easy to drive, functional without any superfluous accessories, light enough to be able to reach sufficiently high speeds yet robust enough to be able to take any type of road. Designed to be simple, with four mechanical units which were easy to access and to understand, the Ford Model T could be repaired quickly and for little cost, since all that was required were standardised parts which could be marketed in local hardware stores. Lastly, the car was sold in several different body versions so as to satisfy the varying needs of Ford's target clientele (Laux, 1982).

During the first two years, total automobile market sales and Ford Model T sales rose at the same pace. Henry Ford's audacity was that instead of maintaining prices in order to fund future investments, he lowered them by 18 per cent. Sales soon reached 56,000 units, three times higher than the year before, whereas total demand had only risen by 33 per cent. Ford pursued this sales price-cutting policy until 1917. By so doing he achieved a volume that was incredible for the time (825,000 units), and dropped his prices to as low as $360 for the touring version of the Model T.

Mass production and lower prices preceded the introduction of assembly line work

The Ford production system did not exist before this acceleration in sales. In actual fact, Ford's system was only invented on a step-by-step basis, and at a much later date than most people imagine. Increased sales volumes soon ran up against the problem Ford experienced in recruiting the skilled employees he needed at the time. Henry Ford, who was not very tuned into the latest manufacturing methods, had the good sense to surround himself with engineers. These were the people who helped him to discover how specialised machine tools could enable him to obtain perfectly interchangeable parts; how he could use workers who had not been particularly trained in this line of work; and how he could save time and labour by organising his factory in such a way as to manufacture and assemble vehicles in a sequential fashion (Sorensen, 1962). The concepts underlying the design of the new Highland Park factory that Ford opened in 1910 included having machines that were specialised in one single operation, and having lines that executed the successive manufacturing and assembly phases (Biggs, 1996).

This did not mean that the issue of the many recently hired and relatively unskilled labourers' work pace had been resolved. Taylor's methods did not provide any particularly long-lasting solutions for a large series production organisation. Drawing inspiration from examples observed in the canning industry, Ford's engineers began testing an assembly line work organisation in 1913, before generalising it in 1915.

By then, production had already reached 395,000 vehicles and the sales price had dropped to $495. It is important to note that mass production and lower unit costs are not necessarily related to assembly line work, i.e., they can be obtained by other means. Similarly, it was not until relatively late that Ford even thought of integrating the entire automobile value chain (from the raw steel to the finished product). He did this in 1920 with a second giant factory that he built on the Rouge River, in the community of Dearborn (suburbs of Detroit). In fact, Ford had been thinking for quite some time that the optimal organisation would entail purchasing components from suppliers and decentralising chassis body manufacturing out to the major sales regions. It was the recurring difficulty Ford experienced in receiving parts from suppliers (in the quantity, quality, time-scale and price he needed) that lead him to design a totally integrated factory.

In sum, Ford's sales prices had to a large extent already dropped before he generalised assembly line work. Moreover, this was a long time before he integrated his production process. This reminder of the timing and of the circumstances involved in the adoption of these processes suggests that neither of them was a logical extension of high-volume production, undertaken purposefully in an effort to achieve greater economies of scale. Instead, they were ways of overcoming the difficulties Ford was facing with the pool of unskilled workers, on one hand, and with his suppliers, on the other. Moreover, these processes caused a sharp rise in fixed costs and created complex problems relating to the breakdown of operations among the various workstations and to the synchronisation of flows.

Uniformisation and integration

Ford tried to overcome these difficulties through even greater uniformisation and integration. He wanted to almost completely standardise both the product and the production. Towards 1917, Ford Model T's were all being manufactured with the same equipment – and they all came in black. Several years later however, variations in demand and lower sales made it necessary to reintroduce greater diversity. Ford systematically recruited young and vigorous production line workers to lessen individual variations in operational speeds – although the labour market did not always allow for this type of recruitment.

Flow synchronisation was also a major concern for Ford. It must be remembered that around 1915 assembly lines were short; that several could be running at any one time; and that they were independent of one another. Moreover, a host of different suppliers was still active. There were as many assembly lines as there were components groups, subsystems and assembly phases within the Ford Model T. With no safety stockpiles being physically located at the head of each line, regular sourcing arrangements had to be made. Workshop managers had to create a new category of workers, 'parts hunters' who were responsible for tracking down parts and components whatever the cost. Ford felt that the only solution to this problem was to create continuous lines, with the upstream section 'pushing' output downstream. He was also convinced of the need to internalise a large number of

Mechanised production line work, parcellisation and structural time loss

They may seem to be congruent, but in actual fact manufacturing and assembly lines differ from the intellectual logic of work – whereas Taylor's method doesn't (Hounshell, 1984).

A mechanised production line infers that a uniform period of time be spent at each workstation (called the work cycle time). This creates a totally new problem. To avoid wasting time or disturbances along the line, operators at each station must execute several operations in an operational time that matches as closely as possible the work cycle time.

To achieve this, operations are deemed to be independent and randomly distributed amongst the workstations. The product's functional logic, which once injected intelligibility into the manufacturing operations' sequencing, disappears. Deprived of any intellectual support, the operator is now forced to memorise operations that are totally unrelated.

A Taylor model preparation of work would break tasks down into elementary operations in order to find the sequence that was supposedly the most efficient and economic (the one best way). However, it did not undermine the intellectual logic of the tasks' execution.

The 'balancing' of these elementary operations amongst the various workstations along the assembly line will never perfectly adjust the operational time (total time necessary to complete the operations allocated to a given workstation) to the work cycle time. The balancing is particularly imperfect when the product is diverse and when peoples' performances are uneven. Operations that include several variations (i.e., a screw that is turned differently and which therefore requires a few more milliseconds) means that the workstation's operational time will have to be increased to reflect this extra time. If it is not possible to obtain from the succession of workers who have been posted to a given workstation that they fulfil its operations with the same speed of execution, the operational time calculation will have to take into account the amount of time that the least performing operator requires.

Moreover, the operations' distribution has to be reshuffled and the balancing recalculated whenever a product modification is introduced – something that occurs frequently. This can lead to longer preparation and explanation times. The line also creates an interdependency between the different workstations, and a problem at one of them has repercussions for the others. The lines stops if an absent person is not immediately replaced; whenever a mechanical incident occurs or a parts supply is interrupted; or when product flows are poorly synchronised between the lines and the trim lines, or interrupted upstream or downstream. In addition, work is disturbed any time that an operation is poorly executed or forgotten.

In the end, lost time, line shutdowns and the extra employees required (replacements, quality controllers, 'reworkers', etc.) can add more than 50 per cent to the theoretical time needed to carry out a particular type of production. Productive models that use mechanised manufacturing or assembly lines are in part distinct because of the way in which they have tried to reduce the time loss that is structurally engendered by a mechanised production line organisation. This is specifically the case for the Ford, Sloan and Toyota models.

Volvo's Uddevalla factory has demonstrated that it is possible to obtain performances that are at least equal to those which can be achieved using a production line even if the work organisation includes teams that build a vehicle whilst operating out of a stationary workstation – as long as the employment relationship is such that it is not in their interest to hinder the sequencing and completion of the work (Freyssenet 1998a, also see chapter 3).

manufacturing operations, and this is what he did at his Rivière Rouge plant after 1920.

Wages are doubled to keep workers from leaving

Long before these attempts to limit production disturbances, Ford had had to cope with a sudden increase in the number of workers who resigned (shortly after the first assembly lines were introduced). To staunch this outflow as quickly as possible, he came up with the solution of an eight-hour workday, paid at a fixed rate of $5. This system was attractive and innovative at three levels: it introduced the eight-hour workday that people had long been demanding; it offered a fixed daily wage; and it doubled average wages. Ford felt that a production line would enable him to predict daily output volumes without it being necessary to resort to variable scheduling. He also thought that it would allow him to impose a certain workflow rate without having to offer performance-related bonuses. Lastly, he felt that the ensuing economies of scale would enable a distribution of profits that was more profitable to his employees (Meyer, 1981).

Ford only theorised the need for regular wage increases (so as to continually broaden demand) once he had become aware of the fact that his 'volume' strategy would only succeed if he extended the Model T's initial customer base of farmers and independent professionals to include a wage earning population. He naively imagined that a simple demonstration of his theory's robustness would persuade other captains of industry to act in the same manner. He did not realise that by triggering a virtuous circle of growth, one that in the 1970s would ultimately be labelled 'Fordist' by the French Regulation School, a nationally contracted wage hike system (and therefore a recognised role for labour unions) would become a necessity. Acting against his own interests, he opposed this system in the name of an authority of employers that he held to be indivisible.

The early crisis of the Ford production system

Ford experienced two alerts, one in 1918 and the other in 1920. His company's sales had fallen much more quickly than total demand had done. With economic recovery, sales rose again, reaching an extraordinary peak of 1.41 million vehicles in 1924. However, this time around Ford's progression was no better than the overall market growth rate. Moreover, the company's profit margins began to come under pressure as the result of a price war that Ford itself had initiated. Even worse, the following year sales began to drop again (reaching 400,000 units in 1927), even as the overall market continued to rise. After a brief turnaround in 1929, output plummeted even further with the advent of the Great Depression. General Motors (and even Chrysler, the rank outsider) moved ahead of Ford, the former permanently, the latter until the Second World War. The Ford 'machine' was beginning to stumble just nine years after the launch of the Model T – and less than three years after the generalisation of assembly lines and the establishment of the $5 workday.

To understand this crisis, we must first examine the pre-conditions that are necessary for the durable viability of a 'volume' strategy. The homogeneous and rising demand that had made a success of the Ford Model T in the United States in fact only lasted for as long as it took the independent professional and high wage earner social categories to develop and to become relatively affluent. Once their incomes and needs started to differentiate, they began to turn to vehicles that were better suited to the changes in their economic and social situations. The vast majority of wage earners were not in a position to replace Ford's initial customers, given the absence of any nationally co-ordinated increase in their purchasing power.

The `volume´-based profit strategy

Out of the six possible sources of profit, a 'volume'-based profit strategy will emphasise economies of scale. Such savings can be obtained from a better spread of fixed costs, i.e., those outlays (investments, product design, workforce training, commercialisation, administration, etc.) that cannot be immediately adjusted to demand levels. The aim is to get such costs to cover as many similar products as possible, for as long as possible. Scale economies lower the cost of each product unit.

In a 'volume' strategy, diversity at most involves having one basic model for each major market segment and for each major automobile market. The product must satisfy the target clientele's essential needs, without any superfluous accessories or finishing that can increase its price. This sort of vehicle sometimes results from an innovative design – which is what occurred with the Ford Model T. However, instead of organising itself in such a way as to design as many innovative models as there are new customer expectations, a firm pursuing a 'volume' strategy will be content to exploit, for as long as possible, the basic model that it had originally designed in order to satisfy what it considers to be the necessary and sufficient needs of the largest number of potential customers. It requires a maximum of regularity and standardisation for its production – an orientation that is contrary to that of an 'innovation strategy', with its need for extensive productive flexibility.

Exceptional conditions of market and of labour

To durably pursue a 'volume' strategy, there needs to be a constantly growing and homogenous demand, as well as a workforce that is abundant and which can be mobilised. It is true that by mass producing a reduced number of standard models that are specific to each major market segment, it is possible to lower prices and to increase the solvency of a greater proportion of the total population. Nevertheless, this extension of the marketplace will soon run into problems if national income distribution is not co-ordinated and relatively egalitarian in nature.

A 'volume' strategy also infers the availability of a growing number of the right type of workers. For this to occur there first of all needs to be sufficient reserves. This can stem from significant under-employment; from certain social categories (rural workers, women, etc.) having assumed wage earner status; from domestic or external population movements; and/or from the localisation of production units in 'emerging' countries from which products and profits can be repatriated without dissuasive taxation. This workforce must also be usable, i.e., it must possess those attributes that are deemed necessary in light of the work organisation that has been chosen.

It is clearly very difficult to imagine a situation in which such market and labour conditions can be observed for any durable period of time at a national (and especially at an international) level. None of the existing modes of growth can guarantee this sort of outcome. This is why it has only been possible to pursue 'volume' strategies, albeit temporarily and exceptionally, during market takeoff phases. The strategy will quickly run into problems, either due to the insurmountable nature of the obstacles found in the type of market that can exist in a growth mode which features a competitive distribution of national income; or else as a result of the social and geographic diversification of demand in distribution modes that are co-ordinated and moder-ately hierarchised.

In theory, the only economies that can durably guarantee those conditions in which a 'volume' strategy can be viable (absence of market uncertainty, homogeneous demand, no alternative products on offer, compulsory employment and work) are the egalitarian regimes of centralised and administrative economies. However, economies of this sort also create a number of obstacles that can impede the strategy's success.

Standard products, a centralised and integrated organisation, rising, high and relatively uniform wage levels

Even after its conditions have all been met, a 'volume' strategy infers that the firm find all of the resources that will enable it to continually achieve economies of scale.

Regarding product policy, such resources must allow a firm to offer, in an ever-greater number of countries, an individual means of transport that can be seen as being necessary and sufficient for a given period of time, both in price and usage terms, either for most of the population or else for each major market segment.

The productive organisation, in design, sourcing, manufacturing and sales terms, must be entirely designed in such a way as to ensure that dedicated facilities can be continually used.

The employment relationship must offer employment conditions that are sufficiently attractive to get people to accept a type of work that consists of endlessly reproducing the same object. Clearly this must also be coherent with the co-ordinated and relatively egalitarian distribution of national income that is indispensable if a 'volume' strategy is to be viable.

To ensure that a firm's players reach an agreement on which means will satisfy the aforementioned requirements, they must all have two ideas in common: that there is a need to make available to the greatest number of people one or several standard product(s) which satisfy the population's essential needs and aspirations; and that it is an appropriate policy to distribute the national income in a co-ordinated and relatively egalitarian manner.

The Ford model

A Ford type of company governance compromise made its appearance at Ford (in the United States) and at Volkswagen (in the Federal Republic of Germany) in the aftermath of the Second World War. It was only from this point onwards that Ford's production system became a Ford model.

Building the Ford model at Ford after the Second World War

Following a ferocious labour dispute during which it had tried to pretend that the automobile workers union did not even exist, Ford was forced to recognise the UAW in 1941 (something that General Motors had done a short time before). Note that General Motors had already become the union's favourite target. Moreover, since it was making the most profits, it yielded more easily to employees' demands. Above all, General Motors' senior management had understood that if the automobile market were to widen, there had to be a generalised and continuous rise in the overall population's purchasing power (see chapter 6). Henceforth, with its de facto consent, General Motors became the benchmark for the other car makers' (and at a wider level, for other American firms') collective bargaining procedures. Wage levels and increases, job classifications, working regulations and social protection – all of these factors became more and more homogenous amongst Detroit's Big Three automakers. Inter-firm competition tended to no longer involve the companies' respective employment relationships – instead, it began to focus on their product policies and productive organisations.

With the vast majority of wage earners being able to access the new car market thanks to this de facto inter-firm co-ordination of social progress, Ford finally found the pre-conditions it needed for its 'volume' strategy. Even as Ford was widening its product range to four models during the 1950s and to seven models during the first half of the 1960s, it maintained its principle of only offering standard vehicles that are specific to each of its major target market segments. It did not try to commonalise its models' platforms – something that General Motors had been doing since the 1930s in its drive to create compatibility between the search for economies of scale and the search for greater diversity. The recent accession of the wage earner social category to the automobile market during the 1950s and the first part of the 1960s allowed Ford to realise volumes of between 300,000 and 400,000 units for each of its models – a production that was almost equal to GM's platform output.

To keep embodying the Ford model (with its limited range of specific models) beyond the first half of the 1960s, Ford had to design models that were also valid in Europe and in Japan. The nationally co-ordinated and moderately hierarchised type of distribution that was being adopted in these regions as well (with the noteworthy exception of Great Britain) theoretically meant that this policy might be a feasible one. However, the varying conditions of automobile utilisation in these regions (and the diverging expectations of the different customer bases) precluded its application. Big, heavy, fuel-guzzling American cars were not appropriate for the European and Japanese markets – and as a result, Ford was forced to adopt a 'volume and diversity' strategy in the United States.

Volkswagen is the second firm to have embodied the Ford model

The authoritarian regimes were all fascinated by the Ford production system. The Nazis had wanted to adopt a matching version. Hitler asked Ferdinand Porsche to design a 'people's car' (Volkswagen) and ordered the construction of an integrated factory at Wolfsburg, imitating Ford's Rivière Rouge plant.

The project was taken up again after the War. Its success was ensured by the Federal Republic of Germany's geopolitical, macroeconomic and social situation. Volkswagen became a State-run firm, with employee and labour union representatives sitting on the Board of Directors. The FRG adopted a mode of growth that was based on the export of specialised products and on a nationally co-ordinated and moderately hierarchised distribution of national income, adjusted to account for the country's gains in external competitiveness.

As a result, German wage earners rapidly replaced independent professionals in their role as purchasers of initial equipment phase entry-level vehicles (like the Beetle). When demand began to shift to larger, more powerful and more comfortable models, it was amplified (and later replaced) by Germany's export markets. In the United States first of all, the Beetle offered a reply (both in price terms and in ease of usage) to demand emanating from women and from young adults. In developing countries such as Mexico and later Brazil, high earning and stable employees (and taxi drivers) could attain this product. For all of these reasons, Volkswagen ended up turning out 15 million Beetles between 1949 and 1973.

This success was quick to impress numerous engineers, leaders and government institutions, especially in countries seeking to develop their own automobile industry. In particular, the Japanese MITI put a great deal of pressure (in vain) on local car makers, asking them to specialise in single market segments and in single models.

During the 1950s and in a number of countries, the Ford model was presented as a one best way, even as the conditions of its viability were beginning to disappear as the result of an automobile market differentiation which was characterised by a moderate hierarchisation of segments. After Ford, Volkswagen also found itself forced to turn to a 'volume and diversity' strategy, and to a Sloan model, so as to overcome the deep profitability crisis it went through just before the first oil crisis erupted.

Is it possible to revert to a 'volume' strategy?

Betting on trade globalisation and on market homogenisation, during the 1980s and 1990s Ford again tried to revert to a 'volume' strategy by pursuing a policy that revolved around offering specific models on each of the world's major market segments. For the moment, this policy would appear to have failed.

Does this mean that a 'volume' strategy is forever damned? A new Ford-type scenario is conceivable in highly populated countries such as China or India, where economic takeoff seems to have begun. Alongside certain recently enriched social categories (which only purchase the major marques' top-of-the-range vehicles), there exists an extremely large population of small farmers, merchants and entrepreneurs whose purchasing power is rising and who have been seeking to move from a 'two-wheel' to a 'four-wheel' means of transport.

The Ford model

The Ford model is a productive model:

1. That implements a 'volume' strategy that is only relevant when national income distribution is relatively egalitarian, or else when this distribution is only differentiated into two or three large and very homogenous social groups, firstly at a national and then at an international level.

2. That fulfils the requirements of this strategy through:

– a product policy aimed at offering a standard model at the lowest possible price to an entire population or to each major market segment;

– a productive organisation that is highly centralised (from design to final sale), sequentially integrated into continuous lines, mechanised and allocated a specific workflow; and based on the pre-determination and standardisation of elementary operations split in an independent and undifferentiated manner between the workstations in such a way as to saturate the work cycle time;

– an employment relationship that offers unskilled workers a fixed wage which is not linked to performance, with regular increases in purchasing power, for a fixed daily work schedule.

3. Thanks to a company governance compromise that is mainly agreed upon by executives and labour unions and which involves allowing people to access mass consumption in exchange for their acceptance of the productive organisation.

6
The 'volume and diversity' strategy and the Sloan model

In the 1920s, General Motors was the first car maker to see that various segments in the American population would soon feel a need for social differentiation (following the rise in their living standards). Above all, it was the first to seek a solution for this turn of events. Neither the 'diversity and flexibility' strategy that GM was pursuing back then nor its production system of the time let it offer, in sufficient volume and at affordable prices, the vehicle product range that people were asking for. The company needed to create compatibility between two sources of profit that at first glance appeared to be incompatible: volume and diversity. Remember that at the time, Ford's mass production of a single car model and other car makers' manufacturing of many different specific models were thought to be two contradictory phenomena.

General Motors found the solution. It used shared parts for its models' non-visible components, and different elements for the visible ones. To make vehicles that were designed in this manner, it invented a new production system that was characterised by the multi-specialisation of the equipment and by the polyvalency of the personnel.

However, the conditions permitting a durable viability for a strategy that combines volume and diversity only cropped up during the 1940s in the United States, the 1950s in Europe, and the 1960s in Japan. The Sloan model that embodied these principles was viewed during the post-war boom years as the productive model that all car makers should be applying. Yet this is a model that was ultimately to experience a number of crises, at different times, and for different reasons, in the United States and in Europe.

An unexpected discovery that resulted from an existing constraint

Durant's ideas at the other end of the spectrum from Ford's

William C. Durant, the man who founded General Motors in 1908, was guided by two main ideas. The first one related to market variability, and to uncertainty about which segments were most likely to develop the quickest. This concept argued in favour of offering an exhaustive range of products, including all types of passenger cars and light commercial vehicles. The fastest way of achieving this goal at the lowest possible cost was to combine, via mergers or acquisitions, a variety of existing marques into a single holding company – so Durant brought Buick, Oldsmobile, Cadillac, Oakland and Chevrolet together under one roof. His second idea was that economies of scale were mostly achieved in the manufacturing of parts. It therefore behoved GM to centralise the production of each part, which would then be dispatched to a decentralised assembly plant located in a region where there was a significant demand for cars (Laux, 1982).

The speed with which the General Motors group was constituted, the autonomy which each of its firms demanded, the difficult implementation of efficient management control systems and the brutal downturn in the economic situation in 1910 and in 1920 – all of these factors meant that on several occasions General Motors was close to going bankrupt. Du Pont de Nemours, General Motors' main shareholder, had Durant voted out. He was replaced by Alfred P. Sloan, who had been heading up the sub-holding that combined General Motors' main parts and accessories companies. Sloan had been noticed because of his management skills and also because of an 'Organisation Study' that had tried to introduce an indispensable coherency into the group.

A 'revolutionary' innovation that endangered the firm's survival

Despite all of Durant's acquisitions, General Motors' product offer did not cover all of the general population's income brackets – and especially not the inexpensive vehicle segment that Ford had been dominating for the past 10 years. Sloan and his executive committee allowed themselves be persuaded by the head of research (the renowned Charles F. Kettering) that the only way to compete with Ford was to offer a car that, in mechanical terms at least, constituted a complete innovation. Kettering claimed to have already begun preparing a revolutionary engine that would quickly leave the Model T far behind. This was an 'air-cooled engine with copper particles mixed into the cylinder walls'. Its supposed advantages were that it could cut the number of parts as well as their weight, thus reducing costs and improving performance. Unfortunately, just a few months before the trumpeted launch of the new vehicle, it was revealed that the engine was not ready yet (Fridenson, 1982).

Sloan urgently gave his Chevrolet division the difficult task of finding a solution. Chevrolet adapted an existing water-cooled engine to the future vehicle's chassis (which had already been designed). It was therefore able to launch the previously announced inexpensive car in 1924, calling it the Chevrolet K. The model was an immediate success, rendering the Ford T obsolete within two years. The main reason for its commercial success was that it made 'inside driving' accessible to all. Despite Henry Ford's opinion that 'outside driving ... was good for the health', 'inside driving' (i.e. cars where the body is enclosed by windowed doors that protect passengers from dust, wind and bad weather) became increasingly popular. Previously such cars had been much more expensive. The Hudson Motor Company had however recently succeeded in lowering its production costs, thanks to new steel sheet stamping techniques – which General Motors was quick to adopt (Kuhn, 1986).

Two lessons to be drawn from this adventure

The achievement and success of the Chevrolet K demonstrated that it was technically possible and commercially acceptable to offer models that are different but which share a number of key elements (i.e., the engine). It also seemed preferable to adapt other manufacturers' innovations quickly instead of assuming this risk alone. GM had just invented the 'volume and diversity' strategy by creating, for the first time ever in the automobile sector, compatibility between these two different sources of profit.

However, if the various models' purchasers were to accept that their cars had certain units in common, the market's previous bipolarisation between expensive and varied vehicles, on one hand, and standardised and inexpensive ones, on the other, had to gradually give way to a demand that was continuously hierarchised. Sloan, who could not resist catchy phrases, would later speak of a 'class' market to describe automobile demand during the first decade of the century; of a 'mass' market for the second decade (the Ford era); and of a 'mass and class' market for the years following (the General Motors era). Although this expression is very evocative, it is nevertheless inaccurate inasmuch as during the interwar period the vast majority of wage earners in the United States were still a long way away from being able to purchase a new vehicle. The 'competitive' distribution of national income that characterised the American growth mode of the time only allowed for a relative and hierarchised increase in independent professionals' and top wage earners' wealth. Moreover, the market hierarchisation that had marked this period, with its lack of any insurmountable barriers between the various segments, was later disturbed by the 1929 Depression.

In the late 1930s, General Motors' executives, more pragmatic than Ford's, understood (in particular because of greater employee demands) that it was necessary and ultimately in their own interest that the American mode of national income distribution be changed. If the demand for automobiles were to extend to all segments of the population and be structured into a continuum that would allow for surface differentiation as well as a deep-seated commonalisation of models, wage hikes would have to be nationally co-ordinated and moderately hierarch-ised (Sloan, 1963). In actual fact, it was during the 1940s that a 'co-ordinated and consumer-oriented' growth mode would replace the 'competitive and consumer-oriented' mode that had previously dominated in the United States. The 'volume and diversity' strategy thus fulfilled the conditions of its durable viability – and the production system that General Motors had gradually put together was able to become a productive model, rightfully as per Sloan.

In the 1950s and the 1960s, most industrialised countries, with the notable exception of Great Britain, adopted the same form of national income distribution as the United States, whether their growth was driven by domestic consumption or by export trade (Boyer, Saillard, 2001). This environment, plus the spectacular results achieved by General Motors, which had become the world's largest industrial group, persuaded many car makers from all across the world to follow in the footsteps of the giant from Detroit. The Sloan model was henceforth presented in schools and in management manuals as the definitive one best way, valid for all firms, whatever their sector of activity. Renault and Fiat got around to adopting it in the 1950s, Ford and Peugeot in the 1960s and Volkswagen in the 1970s.

Chrysler and Nissan, however, were not able to implement it with any real efficiency. Nor was it the only productive model to be applied during the post-war boom years. The 'specialist' car makers continued to pursue their 'quality' strategy. Toyota and Honda were inventing productive models of an original nature at this very same time. Lastly and above all, the Sloan model experienced a crisis that broke out at General Motors and Ford in the late 1960s, and at Fiat, Renault and PSA in the 1970s – before reviving and again prospering at Volkswagen (Freyssenet et. al., 1998b).

To understand the shaping, extension, crisis and resurgence of the Sloan model, it is necessary to carry out a systematic examination of the pre-conditions for (and requirements of) the 'volume and diversity' strategy.

The 'volume and diversity' strategy

A combination of volume and of diversity

The 'volume and diversity' strategy consists of achieving economies of scale by using a maximum number of shared parts in different models; and of broadening demand by differentiating these models on the basis of those parts that the customers view as being distinctive.

There are several ways to get this result. General Motors and the firms that imitated it chose to commonalise the platform, i.e., the chassis (or when this is replaced by an integral body, everything to be found below the body shell), and to differentiate models by body types, interior fittings and accessories. One variant of this principle is to commonalise non-visible parts and diversify visible ones. In recent years there have been a number of attempts to apply this principle. Some car makers have sought to achieve a certain percentage of shared parts, whether visible or not. Others have tried to obtain differentiated models by using a limited number of modules.

In the 'volume and diversity' strategy, quality plays a secondary role. It suffices that the competition's average quality levels are matched (or slightly exceeded if the market is in a product renewal phase). Similarly, innovations need not involve anything more than accessories, fittings or style. Still, architectural or design innovations by car makers pursuing an 'innovation and flexibility' strategy (see chapter 8) must be copied rapidly when sales indicate that they are being adopted by traditional market segments or that they have created durable new segments. Unlike the volume strategy, the 'volume and diversity' strategy requires a certain amount of productive flexibility. However, here flexibility only relates to the facilities' and employees' polyvalency, hence to their ability to manage variations in the demand for the different models, versions and options. As for the sixth source of profit, the permanent reduction of costs at constant volumes, this does not operate as a permanent regime, rather it materialises on an ad hoc basis through the substitution of capital for labour, or else by localising in zones where labour costs are lower.

A moderately hierarchised demand and a polyvalent workforce

Whereas a 'volume' strategy depends on a continual extension of demand if it is to be viable, a 'volume and diversity' strategy can be pursued in a product renewal market as long as there is an increase in the number of parts being shared amongst the various models. It does not matter whether these models are manufactured by the same car maker, by the firms it has absorbed, or by its competitors (through a joint production of parts or through using the same components suppliers).

However, increased commonalisation is only possible in the presence of a moderately hierarchised type of demand. Buyers must accept that it is normal to pay different prices for models in which many elements (frequently the most costly ones) are shared. They must also feel that the models' surface differentiation justifies their own economic and social differences. It is only when income and status differentials between the various social classes are minimal that this does not apply.

As for the workforce, it must be able to master the products' diversity plus variations in the demand for each of them (given that there are so many different options).

These market and labour conditions are especially present in growth modes that are accompanied by a co-ordinated and moderately hierarchised distribution of national income. Inequalities in income and in wealth are limited and gradual in such modes. Professional mobility and upwards social mobility is feasible for a large part of the population. The products' surface differentiation and deep-seated commonalisation are ultimately a reflection of a hierarchised and permeable social structure.

The 'volume and diversity' strategy is also possible (but only temporarily so) in a 'competitive and consumer-oriented' mode. Here the increased wealth of certain social categories spawns a demand that is broader in nature and more hierarchised – as was the case in the United States before the outbreak of the Second World War. However, the exclusion of great masses of wage earners from the market for new vehicles (and the brutal economic and social adjustments this mode of growth entails) means that no durable viability is guaranteed with a 'volume and diversity' strategy.

Commonalisation of parts between the various models, control over product variety, moderate wage hierarchisation and the possibility of career development

Once the conditions that ensure the relevancy of a 'volume and diversity' strategy have been met, it remains to determine which means can fulfil its requirements.

The product policy must find the right balance between diversity and volume. As such, it must offer a vehicle range in which many components are shared; cover the main market segments and types of automobile utilisation; and add to the product range those new vehicle types that are being launched by firms which have opted for an 'innovation and flexibility' strategy (once they have turned out to be durably successful). This often excludes models at the very bottom- or top-of-the-range, or 'niche' products that suit customer categories that are too small in number and of uncertain longevity. Style and accessory-related innovations must be based on sophisticated market studies and carried out by small steps so that commercial relevancy can be tested at each stage. Quality should not exceed the level each social category really needs (given the state of existing competition).

The productive organisation must be such that it is possible to manage the diversity of (and variations in demand between) the different models, versions and options. Here the firm is running two main risks. The first is that it will find itself simultaneously in a situation of under- and over-capacity, depending on the product concerned. In this case, the firm must find a production management system that allows it to smooth out its factory workloads, to better split production up between its workshops (depending on demand) and even to improve the product mix. It therefore needs machines and employees that are highly polyvalent. The second risk is that the production system becomes increasingly complex and that costs get out of control. Diversity can lead to an increase in the number of supply sources, rising inventories, logistical confusion and a proliferation of design departments, administrative services and sales networks. The firm must therefore build a form of organisation that finds room for decentralised management even as it works to ensure overall co-ordination.

The employment relationship must value employees' polyvalency so that this becomes an acceptable outcome for everyone concerned. It must allow for a moderate hierarchy of wages and a sufficient level of professional mobility. This is so that it can be coherent with the type of national income distribution that is necessary if a 'volume and diversity' strategy is to remain relevant.

The economic players who must find a way to fulfil the aforementioned requirements are mainly the firm's executives; employees (through their labour unions); suppliers; and public authorities who guarantee a moderately hierarchised distribution of national income. Shareholders and banks, both of whom are guaranteed a modest but steady remuneration of their invested capital, are generally less directly involved.

The Sloan model

The Sloan productive model was devised both gradually and pragmatically, incorporating market as well as employee expectations – unlike the Ford model, which imposed norms upon both of these categories (Sloan, 1963).

Rise in wage purchasing power vs. increases in productivity

General Motors helped to homogenise wage structures throughout the entire American automobile industry. Faced with rising union power, General Motors recognised UAW in February 1937, and in the 1940s and 1950s signed a series of collective bargaining agreements that set at least four components of the employment relationship. First of all, wages were to be negotiated with the unions on a multi-annual basis. These agreements could be revised, depending on changes in retail price levels and on a pre-programmed rise in purchasing power. This latter target was set in such a way as to reflect gains in productivity. The UAW later got General Motors to offer additional social benefits, due to the overall paucity of the American welfare system. The most spectacular example of social progress occurred in 1955, with the creation of income guarantees that stabilised workers' resources if they were temporarily made redundant. This was a highly unusual benefit for workers to enjoy, given the strongly cyclical nature of American economic activity until that point. Lastly, seniority was recognised as a key criterion for dismissals and re-hirings, replacing the arbitrary nature of previous decision-making (Kochan et. al., 1994).

Parallel product ranges; shared platforms; superficially differentiated models; different body versions; numerous optional accessories; annual modifications

The product policy of the Sloan model consisted of offering under different brand names complete ranges of models that shared common platforms and which were differentiated in style, body, internal fittings, accessory levels and number of options. In addition to this variety, there were also annual modifications that were intended to track customers' changing tastes and income levels as closely as possible, convincing them to buy a new vehicle as often as possible by ensuring that their old one lost value quickly on the used car market. Innovation was limited to improvements in vehicle performance, increased comfort and safety-related or stylistic novelties.

Strategic centralisation and operational decentralisation; creation of subsidiaries and subcontracting; multi-specialised assembly lines; polyvalent employees

To reduce the risks of product diversity, the firm's General Management is structured into two levels. On one hand, there is a centralised strategic management team that defines the Group's main orientations with help from its central services and expert committees. On the other, there are the operational divisions that correspond to its marques and subsidiaries. These implement the strategic choices that have been made in a manner that is appropriate to them.

The marketing, research and development and design departments are strengthened in an effort to track the many different changes in market demand as closely as possible (making sure all the while that the necessary economies of scale are achieved). Towards this end, the design department is organised into a matrix-like structure, i.e., by mechanical parts and subsystems and by vehicle projects.

At the manufacturing and assembly levels, diversity-related risks involve a tangible rise in the time wasted along the production lines; an increase in the number of errors and defects; and costlier mechanisation and automation processes. The Sloan model limits these risks, first of all by outsourcing a number of manufacturing operations and by creating competition between suppliers, whether they are subsidiaries or independent components makers. It then uses assembly lines whenever it is possible to mix the different versions of a given model, or even different models that share one and the same platform. However, these lines (and the tools that correspond to them) should not be thought of as being 'universal'. Very simply, they are multi-specialised. Buffer stocks are introduced where necessary to compensate for the varying times that are required to make the various versions and/or models. The competency that workers need to offer essentially turns on their application of the operational mode variants that correspond to the product mix. They must also be able to shift workstations if the mix changes.

The operations that need to be carried out along a Sloan assembly line, albeit more varied than on a Ford line, are just as pre-determined and randomly distributed amongst the different workstations. The necessary polyvalency not only does not reintroduce the logic of the object that is being built – it renders this logic even more invisible, despite the fact that it is a pre-condition for deploying the operator's intelligence.

Crisis and resurgence of the Sloan model

Far from representing the highest form of capitalism, as many people were quick to affirm in the euphoria of the consumer society, the 'co-ordinated and consumer-oriented' growth mode and the Sloan productive model suffered a crisis that was due to their own internal dynamics and contradictions.

The Sloan model

The Sloan model is the productive model that:

1. Implements a 'volume and diversity' profit strategy that is particularly relevant when income distribution is nationally co-ordinated and moderately hierarchised.

2. Fulfils the requirements of this strategy by:

– a product policy that consists of offering (under different brand names) parallel ranges of models which share a large number of mechanical parts and units and which are differentiated in style, body type, internal fittings and accessories;

– a productive organisation that centralises strategic choice; decentralises responsibility for its implementation at the divisional or subsidiary levels; creates competition between suppliers; uses multi-specialised machines and production lines with buffer stocks; and relies upon a polyvalent workforce;

– an employment relationship that ensures a regular growth in the purchasing power of wages; plus an extension of social benefits and of career development possibilities in exchange for a polyvalent type of work where pay depends on the level and on the number of workstations that are likely to be necessary.

3. Thanks to a company governance compromise that is mainly agreed between management and one or several powerful and recognised labour unions – shareholders being guaranteed a constant (albeit relatively moderate) remuneration of their capital.

The success of growth modes that have a co-ordinated and moderately hierarchised distribution of national income – and the paradoxical consequences for the `volume and diversity' strategy

The growth modes' very success exhausted one primary source of economies of scale – and raised questions about the national labour compromise. This was the situation in the United States during the latter half of the 1960s.

The generalised rise in the standard of living allowed households to equip themselves with automobiles at a relatively rapid pace. Within 20 years, the market reached a product renewal stage. To continue to achieve economies of scale, those car makers who had been pursuing a 'volume and diversity' strategy were forced to turn to new markets, ones that were still in their initial equipment phase. At the same time, these new markets had to accept the fact that the car models they were being offered shared platforms with models from the original market. This was the obstacle that the American automobile producers had to face in Europe and Japan.

However as we have already seen, internationalisation is not the only solution possible. In fact, one of the main ways in which a 'volume and diversity' strategy differs from a 'volume' strategy is that it allows for new economies of scale, even after the markets have moved into a product renewal phase. The only pre-condition is that these markets must remain moderately hierarchised. In fact, it is possible to pursue parts commonalisation through an increase in the number of models per platform; by using components that are shared with competitors; or by merging with or taking over another manufacturer (this latter solution being out of the question when anti-trust laws can be invoked, as was the case in the United States).

The second consequence of the success of the 'co-ordinated and consumer-oriented' growth mode was its modification of those social conditions that had enabled a national labour compromise to take shape. Full employment, rising standards of living, improved social benefits, children's education and upwards social mobility – all of these factors create new aspirations which could mean that previous work methods become unacceptable. Indeed, it was at this point that the Sloan model's company governance compromise experienced a crisis. The utilisation of an immigrant workforce was able to temporarily delay this crisis. However, in the medium term, a 'volume and diversity' strategy can only be pursued if a new compromise is built, and if it brings another type of employment relationship to roost – in short, if a new productive model is invented.

The Sloan model's crisis in the United States – a crisis of productivity and of work

To continue to achieve economies of scale, General Motors, Ford and Chrysler first tried to penetrate 'new' countries including Brazil, Argentina, Australia, South Africa and India – as well as those markets in Europe and in Japan that found themselves in an initial equipment phase. The results were disappointing in the 'new' countries. In addition to the import substitution policies being practised there (an anathema to American car makers, forced to produce and reinvest locally), such markets never became large enough to generate significant economies of scale. Despite the industrialisation measures that these 'new' countries took, their growth modes remained 'inegalitarian and rent-oriented' (see chapter 2).

The outlook was much more promising in Europe and Japan. In Europe, General Motors and Ford owned large subsidiaries, and Chrysler bought several English, French and Spanish firms in the 1960s. However, to re-achieve economies of scale, the Big Three would have had to commonalise their model platforms on both sides of the Atlantic. This turned out to be impossible, due to the significant differences in customer expectations and in the conditions of automobile usage. As for Japan, its market was supposedly opened up once the country joined the OECD and GATT in 1962, but in fact it remained impenetrable. To compound this, local Japanese firms locked up their shareholder structures, meaning that none could be taken over.

The slow down in productivity growth (and thus in distributable gains) caused tensions to rise between the various players involved in this Sloan compromise. Business leaders resisted demands for wage hikes; there was a slowdown in hiring; and professional mobility ground to a halt, with the end result that skilled jobs were increasingly carried out by black workers, a category that began to benefit from the process. The rapid success of America's 'co-ordinated and consumer-oriented' growth mode (and of the Sloan model) paradoxically led to a crisis of work that matched the social crisis of the late 1960s and early 1970s. The monetary and oil crises that followed were enough to bring the whole building down.

Car makers from countries where growth was export-driven (the Federal Republic of Germany, Sweden and Japan) benefited from the deep-seated changes in the American market that were caused by these successive crises. They began to offer their own vehicles, sometimes with spectacular success.

France and Italy: a crisis in the company governance compromise that was followed by a crisis of productivity

Given that solvent demand was far from being saturated in Europe and in Japan, the Sloan model could continue to be applied in favourable conditions here. The problems that ensued later on stemmed first of all from work-related phenomena. Vigorous economic growth had lead to full employment and to a great deal of tension in the labour market, with employees in certain countries using this situation to criticise the way in which work was being organised.

The redrafting of existing company governance compromises became a realistic proposition. The outcome of the debates and conflicts that occurred at the time was not pre-ordained, as the various work reorganisations that took place could conceivably have inspired new compromises. However, this entire process was killed off by the 1974 oil crisis. The sudden slow down in economic growth (and subsequently in the demand for automobiles) hampered the search for economies of scale. This scenario was first played out in the United States, then in France and Italy – but for quite different reasons. One after the other, Fiat, Peugeot and Renault experienced a financial crisis in the early 1980s, following unsuccessful attempts at internationalisation and external growth during which they had tried to rebuild economies of scale or rearrange their company governance compromises in such a way as to cut overall payroll costs.

The rise of the 'co-ordinated and export-oriented' growth mode countries — and the revival of the Sloan model in one of them

Even though the Federal Republic of Germany, Sweden and Japan featured the same form of national income distribution as the United States, France and Italy, they were better prepared to confront, and to benefit from, an international competition that had suddenly intensified in the aftermath of the two oil crises. The FRG and Sweden featured a type of growth that was driven by the export of specialised goods, whilst Japan's growth was based on the export of mundane but inexpensive goods – but all three countries had long linked wage hikes to external competitiveness rather than to internal productivity. The global economic slowdown allowed countries and firms that were already internationally competitive to increase market share. They were able to avoid both the crisis in productivity and the crisis in labour.

This favourable environment allowed Volkswagen to successfully shift from a Ford to a Sloan model in 1974, even as everywhere else this latter model was in crisis. Volkswagen resolutely and immediately commonalised the platforms used for the car models being made by the marques (Audi, Seat and Skoda) that it successively acquired. It emphasised job preservation and reduced working times instead of wage increases. By so doing, and due to the appropriateness of the choices it made, Volkswagen's employees could have the best of both worlds.

Restructuring: a fascination with Japanese success

The Sloan model firms that found themselves in a crisis situation implemented drastic plans, reducing staffing levels and shutting down a number of factories. They were generally in favour of whatever wage deregulation policies they felt could help them achieve recovery. Fascinated by the Japanese car makers' success, they often declared in the 1980s that they wanted to copy such production methods – yet had no clear vision of the diversity involved or of the underlying conditions of viability (Boyer, Durand, 1998). It was only in the late 1990s that such factors became apparent.

Chrysler and later on Renault abandoned the 'volume and diversity' strategy, replacing it with an 'innovation and flexibility' strategy (see chapter 8) that was more in tune with the United States' (and to a lesser extent, with Europe's) shift to a more 'competitive' distribution of income. As we saw in chapter 4, Ford tried to revert to a 'volume' strategy, but without success.

The future of the `volume and diversity´ strategy and of the Sloan model

In the end, the finely hierarchised market of the post-war boom years was replaced by a much more heterogeneous type of market. Starting in the 1980s in the United States and in the 1990s in Europe and Japan, those segments of the population that had benefited from a more 'competitive' and decentralised distribution of income showed great demand for conceptually innovative models: pickup trucks, recreational vehicles, minivans, off-road vehicles, sports utility vehicles, etc. By 2000, market share for these sorts of vehicles had risen to between 25 and 50 per cent, depending on the Triad country concerned. However, it was difficult to use traditional car platforms as a basis for the new vehicles' design. Their technical and commercial requirements are very different from one another, and will become even more so if economic and social inequalities continue to rise. A 'superficial' differentiation, in and of itself, will not satisfy people who want to display their own good fortune and original lifestyle through the motor vehicle they own.

General Motors, Ford, Fiat, PSA and Nissan unsurprisingly copied (as per the tenets of the 'volume and diversity' strategy they still pursue) the conceptually innovative models that Chrysler, Renault and Honda launched once they felt secure that these models would be a durable success. This copying has even allowed General Motors and Ford to become profitable again, in an environment of economic recovery.

The 'volume and diversity' car makers are still faced with a dilemma. The models they have copied have become mundane, and will no longer offer the same sorts of profit margins in the future. Moreover, such models do not create economies of scale that are significant enough to compensate for the fact that their profit margins are lower than is usual with a novelty product – a consequence of firms' difficulty in commonalising their platforms with the platforms of traditionally hierarchised cars.

Is it now the turn of the 'volume and diversity' car makers to take up the gauntlet of conceptual innovation, so as to benefit from the considerable rent it offers for a while? Some of these manufacturers seem to be interested in this possibility, and have been allocating the task to one of their marques. It remains that since the birth of the automobile industry, no one has ever succeeded in carrying out two different profit strategies for a significant period of time. The requirements are far too contradictory.

Still we should envisage the possibility that the current coexistence between the 'competitive and decentralised' distribution of income that tends to dominate in the private sector and the 'co-ordinated and moderately hierarchised' distribution that is mainly preserved in the State sector might last. Are car makers now facing the challenge of having to create compatibility between sources of profit that would on the surface appear to be incompatible (i.e., 'volume and diversity' vs. 'innovation and flexibility')? Has the time come for a major new strategic invention? Is it possible that modular vehicle design will enable economies of scale whilst allowing for the design of new vehicle types involving varying combinations of basic modules?

The other path, possibly a more realistic one, consists of arranging alliances or of acquiring or merging with other car makers so as to commonalise normal or mundane platforms. General Motors and Fiat have been trying to do this ever since they announced an alliance of their European and 'emerging country' models. In its own way PSA has been trying to do the same thing by signing a number of ad hoc co-operative arrangements: with Fiat for the production of passenger vans that are aimed at the upper market segments; with Toyota for the production of a small car; and with Renault and Ford for engine production. Volkswagen has continued to follow a Sloan model path, even if its acquisition of certain very top-of-the-range marques (Bugatti, Lamborghini, Rolls-Royce) has slightly blurred the meaning of its strategy.

7

The ‘permanent reductions in costs’ strategy and the Toyota model

Only two automobile firms have pursued a 'permanent reduction in costs' strategy since World War II: Peugeot and Toyota. One abandoned this path during the 1960s, but the other kept it and even turned it into an original model – the Toyota model. Often inaccurately confused with the Honda model in a construct some observers call the 'Japanese' model, and later theorised under the heading of lean production, it has been presented as one best way for the 21st century. But even though it was supposed to 'change the world' (Womack et. al., 1990), it did not prevent the country where it was allegedly born, Japan, from falling during the 1990s into an economic quagmire from which it had still not recovered by 2001. And even before this, Toyota was forced to carry out deep-seated changes in its production system so as to overcome a crisis of work that for a long time went unnoticed outside of Japan.

The conditions underlying a 'permanent reduction in costs' strategy (and the requirements thereof) help us to understand why it has not been adopted by a even greater number of car makers.

The ‘permanent reduction in costs’ strategy

The 'permanent reduction in costs' strategy is a source of profit because it allows for increased profit margins even as the same volume, diversity and quality is being produced. It can be achieved in various ways: by use of machines that are more rapid, precise and specialised and which therefore allow for lower staffing levels and training time (i.e., by a substitution of capital for the labour); by reduced 'waste' in all areas (labour, materials, energy, tools, investment, etc.); by improved product manufacturability; by lowering supply costs (getting component makers to compete with one another); by a delocalisation of production to countries where costs are much lower; by a sudden reduction in fixed costs via outsourcing (or selling loss-making activities) in such a way as to eliminate over-capacities, etc.

A penny saved is a penny earned

A 'permanent reduction in costs' strategy entails saving financial, material and human resources in all situations. It is based on the idea that nothing is ever certain or stable. A regularly rising demand is subject to fragile social compromises; a product launch can always fail; social conflicts can never be totally excluded; governmental policy can always change; currency rates may be subject to great volatility, etc.

The other profit sources only manifest themselves as an adjunct, wherever they are feasible, useful and compatible. They will also only be exploited if they do not compromise the permanent cost reduction effort. When demand rises sharply, volumes only increase gradually and within the confines of the firm's own financial resources. To avoid premature investments, the only time that diversity rises is when this is what the market demands. Non-quality may be expensive, but so is quality that the customer is not able to notice. Quality must therefore be set at the level that is necessary to be commercially competitive. Not only is innovation not a priority, it should be avoided because of the risks it engenders. However, once the market validates an innovation, it should be copied. Lastly, productive flexibility simply means catching up as rapidly as possible with whatever production plans could not be fulfilled as a result of whatever unforeseen circumstances and breakdowns may have occurred. There is no search for an immediate adjustment of production plans to demand levels. This is because of the immediate costs that such adjustments bring, expenditures that contradict the patient efforts being made to cut costs.

Restrictive market and labour conditions

This strategy may seem optimal, in that it is explicitly designed in such a way as to accommodate economic turnarounds. Yet it is only totally relevant in two situations: in case of a 'shortage and investment-oriented' growth mode (see chapter 2) where the demand for automobiles is limited and the workforce forced to accept the postponement of a higher standard of living; and in the 'co-ordinated and price export-oriented' growth mode, when the market has moved into a product renewal phase, and where the workforce operates under a constraint of having to produce goods that are competitive in international pricing terms.

In the end, this cautious approach to hiring, investment and purchasing may be counter-productive if the growth mode guarantees a sustained long-term rise in demand, and if the workforce is sure to benefit from the distribution of productivity gains and therefore from rising purchasing power. Vehicle unit costs are lowered due to an exhaustive and immediate exploitation of economies of scale, and this drop is much greater and more rapid than that which can be obtained through a simple precautionary control of costs. Firms pursuing a 'permanent reduction in costs' strategy are sometimes subject to a very severe competition that can ultimately endanger their survival – competition from firms following a 'volume and diversity' strategy. This was the situation in which Peugeot found itself in the 1960s.

The 'permanent reduction in costs' strategy is very difficult to implement in growth modes where a 'competitive and decentralised' income distribution prevails. This is because in order to respond to increased demand for conceptually innovative vehicles (and to mobilise a workforce that is focused on career and income opportunities), the financial, commercial and social risks that need to be taken are incompatible with a continuous and planned reduction in costs. This is the dilemma that Toyota seems to be facing in a number of different countries as the new century dawns.

A strategy with stringent requirements, especially in terms of organisation and the employment relationship

The means that have to be found if a 'permanent reduction in costs' strategy is to be implemented are ones that drive costs down to a level that is necessary and sufficient if a company is to be able to show competitive prices in a given environment.

The product policy must satisfy a clearly identified demand, copying conceptual innovations once the average customer has adopted them, and above all gaining new customers and ensuring their loyalty through pricing, quality and delays. This latter requirement constitutes a particular constraint for the productive organisation and for the employment relationship.

The productive organisation must be such that it is possible to achieve savings in all areas and forms of activity (i.e., time, stocks, defects, breakdowns, investments, funding, etc.). At both extremes of the spectrum, one can view a permanent cost reduction programme as the work of an ad hoc committee of executives and technicians – or as something that employees carry out themselves.

In both cases, the employment relationship must be such that people will accept the obvious, immediate and ongoing consequences of this strategy for their employment situation. Where employees participate in the cost reduction efforts, incentives must be offered for meeting the savings targets.

Toyota alone has successfully devised a productive model that provides a coherent response to the aforementioned requirements. Peugeot was unsuccessful when it tried to pursue a 'permanent reduction in costs' strategy during the 1950s and early 1960s.

One gives up, the other perseveres

The priority after the War was to rebuild and to invest in those countries that had suffered heavy damage. Growth in household purchasing power was set for a later date – meaning that there was no guarantee that a mass consumption of passenger cars would develop in the long run.

The absence of any external competitiveness constraint: Peugeot

For these reasons, and after a long series of internal debates, Peugeot opted for a profit margin-based policy instead of a volume-oriented one, positioning itself on a market segment that had been left free between the Renault 4CV and the Citroën 11 CV (a front traction car). Peugeot launched the 203, a 7hp vehicle aimed at a clientele of independent professionals and mid-level managers, thereby providing some continuity with the 1930s. This car, which was the firm's only model until 1955, may have been broken down into several body versions, but this does not mean that Peugeot had turned into a Ford model company. In and of itself, a single model is not the criterion of a 'volume' strategy, much less a Ford productive model. The 203's annual output never exceeded 100,000 units. Peugeot was primarily seeking to lower its cost price continually so as to maintain profit margins, regardless of production volumes. It saved money on purchasing, on the consumption of materials and on indirect labour costs; limited risks related to matters such as capacity, innovation, exportation and overseas facilities; and did everything possible to become self-funding. Highly concentrated and deeply embedded in a predominantly rural region, Peugeot also felt that it was responsible for its employees' jobs, expecting in return that they be loyal to the company and contribute actively to its results – all traits that are the very opposite of a 'volume' strategy and Ford model (Loubet, 1995).

Still, the employment relationship at Peugeot could not remain untouched by the social context of the era (from 1955 through 1965). This relationship was at odds with the prevailing national labour compromise (a co-ordinated and moderately hierarchised rise in the purchasing power of wages that depended on gains in productivity). Peugeot tried to combine this principle with the idea of linking bonuses to the firm's prosperity. Such bonuses could reach 15 to 20 per cent of wages.

In 1959, after an initial slowdown in economic activity, the system (which had been accepted by three minority labour unions in 1955) led to a drop in purchasing power and caused a wildcat strike. Peugeot reacted as if it had the right to unilaterally abrogate the system, whereupon it entered a protracted period of recurring conflicts. Peugeot had not been able to build an employment relationship that was coherent with its 'permanent reduction in costs' strategy or with the 'co-ordinated and consumer-oriented' growth mode that was just beginning to predominate in France.

In addition, although Peugeot was very profitable, it was not growing as rapidly as other car makers who had opted for a 'volume and diversity' strategy. With the opening of national borders (and the new groupings being discussed in the automobile industry back then), Peugeot ran the risk of being marginalised. It therefore decided to change gear and adopt the Sloan option that had been so triumphant in the United States (and that had also lead to the success of Renault, which had far and away become France's leading car maker). Earlier caution was replaced by an external growth policy that only materialised at first through an alliance with Renault involving the production of shared mechanical units – but that later lead to the takeover of Citroën in 1974 and of Chrysler–Europe in 1979.

A social conflict and a limited market: Toyota

Unlike Peugeot, Toyota did not renounce its initial strategy. The paradox is that a 'permanent reduction of costs' was not the preferred strategic orientation of Kiichiro Toyoda, the firm's founder and a fervent admirer of Ford. However, the situation in the late 1940s precluded a 'volume' strategy. The demand for passenger cars was set to be durably limited – and in actual fact, the investment and savings-oriented growth mode that Japan had been forced to adopt after the War lasted until the early 1960s. Toyota had to find a way to be profitable without relying on economies of scale. It opted for a permanent reduction of costs, and first and foremost, of personnel costs.

However, Toyota had already had to make a commitment that was seemingly at odds with this target – to wit, the maintenance of its staffing levels. In the late 1940s, the American authorities (who had been overseeing the Japanese economy since 1945) imposed a deflationary austerity policy on the country. Toyota's labour union, worried about the job situation, had been guaranteed by Kiichiro Toyoda that no one would be fired without warning. However, when the financial situation began to degenerate rapidly, Toyota had to turn to a banking syndicate that demanded that it impose an immediate redundancy programme. This lead in 1950 to a social conflict that ended with the departure of the firm's founder. Tensions continued despite a rapid return to profitability resulting from military and civil orders related to the Korean War. To restore social peace, Toyota made a commitment to its employees' job security, and to developing their careers (Cusumano, 1985).

The Toyota model

The Toyota model stems from a process that makes it possible to resolve the contradiction between a production system whose organisation had been entirely based on the reduction of costs, and an employment relationship that guaranteed jobs and career development (Shimizu, 1999). The solution that was gradually developed during the 1950s was formalised in 1962 in a 'joint management–union declaration'. Employees accepted to participate directly in cost reduction efforts to ensure the firm's competitiveness and to gain market share. In exchange, they were offered a management system that guaranteed job security and career development for existing staff. This was a company governance compromise that prioritised longevity – both for the firm and also for jobs.

Traditional and well-equipped products without any superfluous diversity

In this context, cost reduction mainly means a product policy that takes no risks on quantity, diversity or novelty, and which does not increase quality any more than that which is strictly necessary from a commercial point of view. Whatever the circumstances, Toyota's output has always risen at a remarkably steady rate. Its basic models have always been well-equipped in order to limit diversity (which can be costly in production terms) and also so as to procure commercial advantages at constant prices. Toyota has stayed away from launching

vehicles whose customer base is neither clearly identified nor sufficiently widespread. It has also been very prudent in terms of its export
initiatives and establishing of overseas facilities. Toyota will only move
into a market once it has observed it for a long period of time.

A just-in-time productive organisation

The search for lower costs regardless of sales volume basically inspired
the technical and organisational innovations of Taiichi Ohno, a manufacturing engineer said to be the father of the 'Toyota production
system' (Ohno, 1990, Shimizu, 1999).

What Ohno called the 'autonomisation' of machines consists of
equipping them with simple and inexpensive shutdown systems if mal-
functions or defects occurred. This allows one person to supervise an
increasing number of machines.

Kaizen partially involves extending autonomisation to the work
teams themselves. They are asked to contribute to the reduction in
standard times (i.e., the times that are initially determined by the
process engineering department for carrying out the various basic operations) by improving their distribution amongst the various workstations, and by simplifying them. Who better than the people who
carry out these operations to eliminate time wastage at the lowest cost?

The *Kanban* labelling system is intended to act upon the second
largest cost item after payrolls, i.e., materials and parts stocks. Optimal
'economic' fluidity is reached when it is possible to avail oneself, on
time and at the desired location, of the quantity, quality and variety of
specific parts that the production plan requires. The daily reality of life
in a workshop includes breaks in production, running out of supplies,
safety stocks, defects, breakdowns, etc. Constantly seeking the least
costly solution, Ohno found a way of synchronising flows without cen-
tralising or automating their management. This was the opposite of
what many other car makers would be doing (notably Nissan in Japan).
Inspired by the shelf stocking systems he saw in American supermar-
kets, he had the idea of triggering parts supply orders as soon as work
had started on the last batch.

He subsequently reduced batch sizes so as to approximate a *just-in-
time* situation. This reduction in batch sizes above all made it possible
to determine which sectors were having problems respecting deadlines
and quality norms. Their difficulties had been previously masked by
the existence of large amounts of intermediary stock. The supply breakdowns that subsequently came to light forced these sectors to resolve
their problems right away, instead of delaying their analysis and search

for solutions. They could no longer just 'live with' their problems. The problems were to be treated, and the work teams' involvement in this activity gradually enabled a reduction in production times.

Lastly, production was *mixed* and *smoothed out* to reduce variations in assembly line workloads caused by the products' diversity and by fluctuations in demand.

Wages that are based on meeting time reduction goals; and an employment guarantee

To encourage workers to participate in this reduction of standard times, Ohno designed a system in which monthly wages and career development depended on meeting, month after month and team by team, targets that were set by the relevant management team. This initiative was closely watched and promoted by work team leaders and by foremen whose salary and promotion possibilities also depended on the results their team obtained (Shimizu, 1999). No other Japanese car maker has ever been able to set up this sort of wage and promotion system.

How was Toyota able to guarantee employment and career development, even (until 1992 at least) regularly increasing its staffing levels in Japan? First of all, it constantly increased its national (and later worldwide) market share thanks to its prudent product policy and maintenance of competitive prices. It also followed an extremely restrictive recruitment policy, limiting the number of employees to a level that was far below that which the firm actually needed. This was achieved through the systematic use of overtime, and by the outsourcing of capacities.

Schedules included two shifts (a day shift and a night shift) that were theoretically separated by four hours of downtime. In reality, this downtime was often used as an overtime period during which Toyota could achieve a level of output exceeding the low hypothesis in its production plan – and/or catch up on any delays caused by system breakdowns or defects. Capacity outsourcing decisions were always taken at a very high level, with nearly half of Toyota's cars being assembled by subcontractors.

Partnerships with suppliers

Cost reduction is a policy that will only offer finite possibilities if a firm's suppliers and subcontractors are not following the same path. Toyota committed itself to guaranteeing its suppliers a volume of orders over a given period and to sharing with them the benefits of cost reduction if they consented to adopt the Toyota production system, especially its just-in-time sourcing of plants and workshops (Shimokawa, 1994). It remains that the firm was always careful to have at least two suppliers for any one part. Partnerships were also accompanied by periodic best performance competitions pitting suppliers against one another.

The heyday of the Toyota model and its subsequent crisis

Once the market had become mass-oriented, Toyota might have abandoned a profit strategy that was putting its employees, suppliers and executives under a lot of pressure. Japan had adopted a 'co-ordinated and price export-oriented' growth mode by the mid-1960s, with a co-ordinated and moderately hierarchised distribution of national income that was adjusted to reflect gains in export competitiveness.

To a certain extent, Toyota also preferred to benefit from the other profit sources that it was able to exploit: economies of scale; product range effects; and useable quality. By maintaining its strategic orientation, it was able to fulfil, with a remarkable efficiency, the mission that

---

The Toyota model

The Toyota model is a productive model:

1. That implements a 'permanent reduction in costs' profit strategy which is particularly relevant in the 'shortage and investment-oriented' and 'co-ordinated and price export-oriented' growth modes.

2. That fulfils the requirements of this strategy through:

– a product policy offering well-equipped basic models in each market segment, without superfluous diversity or novelty, with plans for constantly rising volumes;

– a just-in-time productive organisation at an internal and external level, intended to reveal and solve right away any problems that might prevent continuous and regular flows and cause wasted time, labour, materials, energy, tooling and space;

– employment and subcontracting relationships that induce employees and suppliers to contribute to the permanent reduction in costs, the former through a pay system in which monthly wages are based on reductions in each work team's standard times, the latter by committing to a volume of orders and to a sharing of gains.

3. Thanks to a company governance compromise that focuses on the firm's longevity, on an employment guarantee and on partnerships with suppliers and subcontractors.

the Japanese government had allocated to the national automobile industry, i.e., to become an export sector capable of driving the country's growth. When the 1974 crisis first broke out, Toyota was ready to face the intensified international competition – and indeed to take advantage of it.

Toyota's competitiveness has been attributed to a 'Japanese model' of which it is allegedly an emblem. History has revealed the lacunae of this theory. Furthermore, and as with any model, the viability of the Toyota model is not without limits. In this instance, the constraints go by the name of social and political acceptability.

The Toyota company governance compromise can only survive under two conditions: employees must continue to accept a reduction in their standard times and an improvement in their performances whilst carrying out a parcellised type of work under severe time constraints (and working a great deal of overtime); and suppliers and subcontractors must continue to lower their prices.

Toyota first faced the difficulty of reproducing these conditions in the United States, when it was obliged to establish facilities in that country. At the beginning of the 1980s, the American government required all Japanese car makers to produce cars locally to obtain permission to increase their sales. Toyota finally consented after a long period of hesitation and after having taken a number of precautions (Shimizu, 1999). Its first step was to develop a joint venture with General Motors, called NUMMI, which took over a plant that GM had been preparing to shut down. Toyota used this experience to test whether it would be possible to come to an agreement with the UAW automobile workers labour union. The UAW, which turned out to be more co-operative than Toyota had expected, accepted its work time and wastage reduction principles in exchange for the firm's commitment to avoid dismissals, maintain an equitable wage structure, and discuss its production plans, schedules and workforce allocations with the union. Nevertheless, Toyota was unable to transplant its wage, career development and scheduling systems to the US. It also had to trim its assembly lines, in the sense that it had to introduce buffer stocks to loosen the constraints caused by the just-in-time organisation (Mishina, 1998). This system, born at NUMMI and copied in Toyota's other US transplants, did not feature the self-regulated and cumulative dynamics of the Toyota model – even though up until that point at least its performances had been very good (Boyer, et. al., 1998).

It was back in Japan that the Toyota model ran into the limits of its social acceptability. The company governance compromise that had spawned the model crumbled in the late 1980s. This took on the form of a work crisis (Shimizu, 1998).

Toyota first met with major recruitment difficulties during the 1986–1990 speculative bubble, when domestic demand rose from three to five million vehicles. It could not attract enough young workers to cope with the rush of orders. In a full employment environment, workforce entrants preferred going into sectors where working conditions were much less difficult (Toyota at the time was making an unacceptable use of overtime). Workers and foremen not only refused to operate under such conditions, but began to raise doubts over the Toyota production system itself.

Toyota's management team, after consulting with its union(s), was forced to change its wage and promotion systems; eliminate overtime at the end of an eight-hour workday; and reintroduce buffer stocks along its manufacturing and assembly lines. Toyota could no longer rely on its operators to reduce their own standard times, and this task would henceforth be delegated to specialised teams. Average monthly wages would be slightly modulated to reflect the realisation of materials and tools savings targets that the work teams would devise themselves. The two day shifts were to work one right after the other, making it impossible to extend the workday through overtime. Annual working hours dropped. Assembly lines were split into segments, separated by buffer stocks so as to return a modicum of autonomy to the work teams (Shimizu, 1998, 1999; Fujimoto, 1999).

Toyota remembered that during the 1960s European firms had gone through a similar crisis of work in a similar environment of rapidly rising demand. Its engineers were particularly interested in Volvo's and Mercedes' experiences, these being the two firms that had made the most progress towards the 'humanisation of work'. They did not directly copy any of the practical solutions that had been used (Mercedes' extension of its work time cycles; Volvo's use of automated guided vehicles at its Kalmar plant; or else Volvo's Uddevalla system with two to four workers assembling an entire vehicle in a stationary workstation [see chapter 3]). However, Toyota did retain the idea that a modicum of intellectual logic should be re-injected into operators' elementary operations. Even though not every operator was able to regain this capacity (due to the intrinsic logic of the production line organisation), Toyota's engineers ensured that each work team had a complete unit to manufacture or to assemble on its own trim line.

Toyota was therefore pursuing a permanent reduction in costs strategy, but by other means. It no longer counted on the employees themselves to reduce their standard items. However, it is by no means certain that the new 'company governance compromise' that developed after this work crisis was as robust and efficient as the one that had previously turned Toyota into the world's third largest car maker.

The future of the 'permanent reduction in costs' strategy

Toyota's executives clearly saw that the traditional type of demand (hierarchised, stable and broken down into four major contiguous segments) was losing ground in all of the Triad countries to a type of demand that was more heterogeneous and volatile in nature. They understood that this trend would create problems for the group's cautious and traditional product policy.

Unsurprisingly, Toyota quickly moved to copy those conceptually innovative models that were most likely to be commercially durable. But it also carried out its own innovations in the late 1990s, launching the first hybrid motor vehicle, the Prius, as well as a vehicle that was specifically targeted at young urban residents.

Was Toyota trying to combine conceptual innovation with something that is even more at odds with this than volume and diversity are, i.e., with a permanent reduction in costs? Will it be able to durably assume the risks that are inherent to this type of innovation, without taking anything away from its previously satisfied priority a permanent reduction in costs? Honda's example demonstrates the extent to which an 'innovation and flexibility' strategy requires a specific utilisation of a firm's financial, material and human resources.

8

The `innovation and flexibility´ strategy and the Honda model

Car makers who arrive late in the automobile sector and who are trying to carve out space for themselves amongst firms with already established market positions often choose to pursue an 'innovation and flexibility' strategy. Examples include Chrysler and Citroën in the 1920s, or Honda in the 1960s. The strategy has also been followed by firms who were having serious problems and who were trying to regain profitability by exploring (or even by creating through their product offer) new market segments: Citroën in the 1950s, Mazda in the 1970s, Chrysler in the 1980s, Renault in the 1990s. Such firms' occasionally spectacular successes have often been followed by failures that were just as resounding. Before attributing (as is often the case in biographical literature) success to one engineer's founding genius and failure to one executive's blindness (or to incomprehension by his/her colleagues or to bad luck or to financial agents' short-sightedness), such successes and failures should be analysed in the light of the conditions in which this sort of strategy can be viable.

The `innovation and flexibility´ strategy

Innovation can only be a source of profit under two conditions. It must be commercially relevant – and better if not be immediately copied (or perfected) by the inventor's competitors. Its success will be all the greater if it affects something that really matters to the target clientele. Different levels of innovation can be distinguished: those that relate to the vehicle's accessories or to its mechanical units, those that change its architecture or style and lastly those that introduce a new concept concerning the product's practical and symbolic utilisation – whether or not this had been asked of previous levels of innovation.

As for productive flexibility, as we have already seen with the 'diversity and flexibility' strategy this will be a source of profit when it enables a firm to adjust its costs to demand variations better and more rapidly than its competitors do. Such responses can range from simple quantitative adjustments to the firm's actual 'responsiveness', meaning its ability to reconvert its operations rapidly (at the design and manufacturing levels) so as to be able to offer products that better satisfy all or some of its customers' expectations.

The unbreakable bonds between conceptual innovation and reactive flexibility

An 'innovation and flexibility' strategy emphasises conceptual innovation and responsiveness to demand. Conceptual innovation is as profitable as it is risky. If the new product on offer is not convincing enough given the potential customer base's practical and symbolic expectations, it is sure to fail. Insofar as it is impossible to be successful always, a car maker who innovates conceptually must organise himself in such a way as to keep the consequences of his inevitable failure to a minimum. He must also be able to abandon quickly, without too much hesitation and for as little cost as possible, any model that has met with little or no public approval. Conversely, when the car maker is successful, it must be able to derive maximum benefits for as long as possible from the rent received from the innovative product, until such time as this product is copied or improved upon by its rivals. Note that competitors will hesitate before attacking the newly created market segment if the innovative firm shows that it is capable of immediately and massively responding to potential demand and that it can improve the product without delay.

Where an innovating firm is capable of this, it can achieve considerable volumes and economies of scale – as long as the market that has been created is broad and covers several countries. This does not mean that the innovator has turned to a 'volume' strategy, much less that it has become a Ford model firm. In reality, its average volumes per model are generally relatively low, since elsewhere it will also be offering innovative models to smaller clienteles. Above all, its objective is not to make profits by lowering the price of some standard model that is supposed to be purchased by as many consumers as possible. Rather it is to create an innovation rent which it can exploit for as long as possible by keeping competitors from upsetting its apple cart.

Models can therefore be very diverse in an 'innovation and flexibility' strategy. On the other hand, quality can be average and even a little below average. People who buy innovative vehicles are in fact taking a relativistic view towards defects that they would not tolerate on a standard vehicle, due to their contentment in having a product with which they identify. Can a permanent reduction in costs enhance the profits that stem from an innovation rent?   This is unlikely since if the priority is to avoid any sudden changes in production rates, logically the firm will reject any conceptual innovation that it considers as being too risky. On the other hand, fixed costs will have to be kept to a minimum to facilitate reconversions of the productive apparatus.

Original expectations that must be satisfied; opportunistic and mobile employees

The 'innovation and flexibility' strategy presupposes a periodic heterogenisation of demand. New expectations and needs must be emerging at regular intervals. The workforce also has to accept rapid conversions from one product to another.

Growth modes featuring a 'competitive' form of income distribution best fulfil these conditions. In actual fact, different or new social or professional groups are periodically strengthened or spawned by this form of distribution, which is based on individual merit, the balance of power and financial opportunism. Here such groups are actually supposed to publicise their new economic and social position, notably through a distinctive automobile demand that satisfies their specific needs.

This is particularly the case in a 'competitive and consumer-oriented' mode. The 'competitive' nature of the income distribution is alleviated by a growth mode that is consumption-driven and which is therefore relatively unconcerned with foreign competition. On the other hand, in the 'competitive and competed' mode, social relations are so fraught and destabilising that the various social categories seek solace in the social and professional positions they have acquired, with everyone trying to reinforce the symbolic expression of his or her specificity. The heterogeneous nature of the demand and the flexible nature of the workforce are turned inside out – the market is 'balkanised', with people falling prey to an inwardly-focused professional rigidity. The 'competitive and competed' mode that was initially beneficial for the 'innovation and flexibility' strategy tends to asphyxiate this strategy as time goes on.

The 'competitive and price export-oriented' mode that characterised South East Asia's so-called 'emerging' countries lead to the development and enriching of an entrepreneurial class and of certain independent professionals – without allowing the other sections of the population to attain, for any durable period of time at least, the threshold of solvency that is required to make new capital equipment purchases. Those who benefit from this mode tend to express their good fortune by purchasing those vehicles that are the internationally recognised symbols of wealth rather than by any specific new demand. This mode, which had initially been relatively unfavourable to the 'innovation and flexibility' strategy, could be beneficial to it if the country involved succeeds in remaining competitive and in expanding and renewing the spheres within which it redistributes its international trade gains.

Even though they constitute a significant constraint on the emergence of new social categories, growth modes that are characterised by a co-ordinated and moderately hierarchised type of distribution do not entirely preclude an 'innovation and flexibility' strategy. The generalised rise in living standards provokes qualitative changes in demand (i.e., increased financial autonomy for young adults and for women, more free time). The labour market may work to the advantage of certain new or existing professional categories, due to a waiving of the common rules that customarily translate into a moderate hierarchisation of income and wealth. But in these sorts of modes, qualitative changes in demand tend to become widespread, and those products that have been able to anticipate such changes tend to be integrated into standard product ranges, and therefore copied by firms pursuing other profit strategies. As for those social or professional categories that have temporarily benefited from this mode, they are gradually reintegrated into the employment hierarchy, as a result of the pressure exerted by other social groups and due to a loosening of their own particular labour market. In other words, new expectations crop up less frequently and are trivialised more quickly – thereby diminishing the relevancy of the 'innovation and flexibility' strategy.

Requirements that are diametrically opposed to those that can be found in a `permanent reduction in costs' strategy

The means that need to be acquired and the company governance compromise that has to be built should make it possible to offer commercially relevant and conceptually innovative products, on one hand, and to dispose of a rapidly reconvertible production tool and workforce, on the other.

The product policy must therefore anticipate new practical and symbolic expectations that have hardly begun to be formulated, emanating from those sections of the population that are just starting to emerge or whose lifestyle has been changed. For this to occur, the first necessity is a direct and finely tuned knowledge of potential clients – something that no conventional market study will have been able to detect or understand. Next, there is a need for a great deal of imagination (along with inventiveness and technical competency) in order to apprehend the form in which the aspirations that have been detected will materialise. Above all, the firm must be capable of launching innovative models that correspond to the market's potential segments – without being impeded or disturbed by other economic players, or by the commitments that may have been made to them (particularly to financial counterparts and suppliers).

At the design level, the productive organisation must include systems that allow for a preservation of innovative capabilities. This can be achieved for instance by hiring innovative persons away from one's competitors, or else by setting up an internal system that detects these types of people and encourages them to express themselves at all levels.

In the manufacturing area, the facilities must be capable of being converted for as little cost as possible – or they must be sufficiently flexible to handle products that, by definition, could not have been foreseen when the facilities were first designed. Not only do the employees have to be polyvalent, but even more importantly they must be able to shift very quickly from one type of production to a completely different one. These requirements also apply to suppliers. A minimum of two solutions are possible: either the manufacturer convinces its suppliers to adopt the same organisation by guaranteeing them a certain volume of orders, or else it does not make any commitments to them, and gets them to pay for a large proportion of the conversion costs.

As for the employment relationship, it must ensure that the measures involved in renewing a firm's capacity for conceptual innovation, and in maintaining a rapidly reconvertible workforce, are socially feasible and acceptable. The traits and competencies that should be stressed during the recruitment, training and work allocation phases are imagination, awareness, initiative, expertise and mobility. The means for enhancing these attributes can range from the complete individualisation of wage and promotion policies to the establishment of collective rules acknowledging the primacy of initiative and expertise.

The main players in the company governance compromise are business executives, innovators and employees. Financial counterparts and suppliers are either excluded, neutralised or allocated a secondary or dependent position. This prevents them from subverting the requisite levels of risk-taking and responsiveness.

Chrysler, Citroën, Honda, Mazda, Mitsubishi and Renault have all at some point in their history followed an 'innovation and flexibility' strategy. Honda alone was able to pursue this strategy durably, fulfilling its requirements through the coherency of the means the firm applied – and thereby inventing a productive model.

Despite being born in Japan, the Honda model is the opposite of the Toyota model

The market and labour conditions required for the success of an 'innovation and flexibility' strategy were far from present in Japan during the 1960s (when national income distribution was co-ordinated and moderately hierarchised). To implement the strategy profitably, Honda turned to the international market, where it found the sorts of clients it needed for its products. By so doing, Honda, in its own way, reinforced Japan's export-driven growth. Moreover, it got its employees to accept an employment relationship that differed somewhat from the national labour relationship.

Genesis of the Honda model

Honda had already devised a productive model before it had even begun to make cars in 1967. A manufacturer of 'two-wheelers' since 1948, thanks to its innovative models, within 12 years it had become the world's leading producer in this field.

Honda pursued the same strategy in the automobile business, thus consolidating its productive model. First of all, it was able to launch at the right time, and in the right place, the sorts of vehicles that were likely to satisfy a rapidly growing demand. It started out by designing a front traction mini car, the N360, for customers who wanted to move from a two-wheeled to a four-wheeled vehicle. It achieved this by equipping its car with an air-cooled two-cylinder engine that it developed into a 31hp motor with a maximum speed of 115 km/h. Honda was the first manufacturer to produce an engine that satisfied the anti-pollution standards the United States was requiring towards the late 1960s. Even before the deadline for adopting these norms, Honda had built a 1500cc engine with reduced exhaust emissions and lower fuel consumption it called the CVCC (Compound Vortex Controlled Combustion). It fitted this engine onto the Honda Civic in 1973, even before the first oil crisis had broken out. This was a compact car that was attractive to a clientele of young adults, particularly in the United States, because it was clean, reliable, slightly sporty, elegant, roomy and came in a number of different body versions. By 1976, one million Civics had been sold across the world. Cumulative sales reached the twomillion mark in 1979, and the three million mark in 1982 (Mair, 1994).

Honda maintained its innovation path. It launched a new engine, the CVCC II, that resolved a contradiction previously considered to be insurmountable, i.e., the engine performed as well as any other yet was cleaner and consumed less fuel than its previous version. In 1984, Honda offered six car models, using four platforms for this. The same year, it exported, or made overseas, 63.4 per cent of its global production.

Engineers at the behest of financiers

Honda's success in the motorcycle business and the astronomical rise of the N360 owed a great deal to Soichiro Honda himself – as did the failure of the following model (the 1300), which seriously endangered the firm. This last model was too noisy, dirty and expensive, the fault lying with the air-cooled engine that Soichiro Honda stubbornly preferred over water-cooled ones (believing that an air-cooled engine would enable greater horsepower for an equivalent engine size). Thankfully, Soichiro Honda's associate Takeo Fujisawa, head of organisation and finance, forced him just in time to reopen research into water-cooled engines, the only type capable of meeting mandatory toxic gas emission and fuel consumption standards. As such, it was against Honda's founder's wishes that the company's engineers developed the CVCC. The success of the Civic turned Honda into a car maker once and for all.

From the very outset, Fujisawa had sought to protect Honda against the risk of losing its ability (and freedom) to innovate in a manner that was relevant and durable. The 'research and pre-project' activity was separated from the product development department and turned into a subsidiary so that it would not be overly dependent on the demands of the design centre. Each engineer was free to submit his/her projects to an assessment committee. If one of these projects were selected, the engineer received a budget and was free to put together his/her own team. Design and research staff recruitment criteria did not prioritise the renown of a job applicant's university, as was the case at Toyota and Nissan. Instead, emphasis was placed on the outcome of a recruitment interview that was intended to detect which individuals were the most imaginative and entrepreneurial. Salespersons were integrated into the innovation process, in that they were allocated the extra task of identifying new market expectations held not only by the firm's clients but also by the population in general

Inventiveness and expertise was also made a priority for all employees, notably via a promotion pathways structure and a wage matrix called the expert system that existed alongside the traditional pathways and matrices. This system, which had been thought up during the 1950s, could not be implemented before 1967 because of union opposition. Nevertheless, measures were taken right away to identify, encourage and support those workers who demonstrated initiative and imagination (Sakiya, 1990).

Staying independent: neither a keiretsu nor an association of suppliers

The freedom to take innovation-related risks also implies that a firm remains independent at the financial, organisational and political levels. Honda did not try to join a *keiretsu* (association of banks and industrials). Quite the contrary, it ensured that its growth was self-funded. Moreover, unlike Nissan, it did not try to develop close ties with politicians. Nor did Honda build up a suppliers' association to which it would have had to make certain commitments – it preferred relying upon Toyota's and Nissan's suppliers, thereby benefiting from their experience and low prices without having to offer anything in return. Finally, it did not turn to Japan's famous trading companies for help with its export drives or when setting up facilities overseas.

Rapid individual promotion vs. responsiveness and initiative

The main players in the company governance compromise that lies at the heart of the Honda model are executives (legitimised by their personal innovative capabilities or ability to enhance other persons' aptitudes in such a way as to benefit the firm and its employees) and the employees themselves (asked to express their personal thoughts on the product or production process [design, manufacturing, sourcing and sales]). This system made it possible to reconcile the firm's innovative capabilities with the acknowledged primacy of employees' individual interests and attitude towards work. The Honda compromise postulates that innovative capabilities can be found, nurtured and enhanced within the firm itself, and that they should not be sought externally (as Chrysler has done). Working within the framework of an organisation that permits this orientation, employees at all levels commit to developing their level of expertise, showing initiative and being imaginative. In return, they enjoy a more reflexive type of work, rapid career promotion based on actual abilities (and not on age, seniority or diplomas), an employment guarantee and good working conditions (specifically the sector's shortest annual, weekly and daily working times). It is hard to imagine a company governance compromise that is more different to Toyota's. Honda has given birth to a productive model that is enacted through means that are completely different to those which characterise the Toyota model.

Innovative products, re-convertible equipment and personnel, a double-edged pay system and better working conditions

The financial performances of a Honda model firm, like the employment guarantee it offers its workforce, basically depend on the commercial relevancy of its product innovation – and on its ability to reply immediately and massively to whatever demand materialises if the product succeeds. This is why product policy, productive organisation and employment relationship are all very marked by such concerns.

The product policy consists of periodically launching models that provide a response to what the new sections of the population expect in those markets where they have made themselves known. The product constitutes a whole that is technically and stylistically coherent. As such, it usually has its own platform, unlike Sloan model cars. The models that are studied and then launched originate in procedures that give designers a great deal of freedom to come up with whatever proposals they want to make. These procedures also permit autonomous work by teams working outside of any hierarchical structure. The teams are built around projects they themselves will have devised and which management will have chosen. All problems are analysed according to at least two different methods.

The productive organisation features very little integration, as well as a production tool that is light and which can be re-converted rapidly. Assembly support tools are preferred to automation whenever the latter compromises the ability to move quickly from one type of production to another, raising the 'break even point' to a dangerous level. This avoids the type of heavy civil engineering work that usually goes along with the installation of major capital equipment – and translates the preference for light and transformable facilities (Freyssenet, 1999a).

The employment relationship attempts to enhance innovation as well as the ability to change products rapidly. Employees are hired, allocated and promoted not in light of their diplomas or age but to reflect the practical and innovative capabilities they demonstrate during extremely long recruitment procedures. The wage system and hierarchical matrix are double in nature: there is a traditional system; and there is a so-called expert system for all those who are committed to developing the competencies they have displayed.

Success is never guaranteed once and for all

The productive model invented by Honda helped the company to cope with the various difficulties that it faced in the early 1990s: tensions in

---

The Honda model

The Honda model is a productive model:

1. That implements an 'innovation and flexibility' strategy which is particularly relevant in growth modes where national income distribution is 'competitive'.

2.1. That fulfils the requirements of this strategy through:

– a product policy that consists of designing conceptually innovative and specific models so as to satisfy the expectations of the new sections of the population; and to produce these models massively if subsequent demand confirms expectations; or to withdraw them without delay if the public is not interested in them;

– a productive organisation that can be reconverted rapidly and for little cost thanks to a low degree of integration; to a production tool featuring low levels of automation and lacking in heavy equipment; and to a personnel that is responsive;

– an employment relationship that highlights individual expertise and initiative in areas such as recruitment, training, wages and promotion so as to nurture within the firm the emergence of competent and imaginative innovators at all levels and in all areas and enhance their ability to move rapidly from one activity to another.

3. Thanks to a company governance compromise that is essentially developed by the executives and employees, and which is based on the firm's remaining financially and organisationally independent from banks and suppliers so as to be able to take those risks that are necessary. Executives are guaranteed that they will be able to benefit inside of the company from the appropriate innovation capabilities and from the indispensable productive flexibility; and employees are guaranteed that they will be able to experience a career development that matches the talents they have acquired, plus that they will enjoy working conditions that are amongst the best in the sector.

---

the labour market; and the failure of several of its models. Although Honda, like the other Japanese car makers, lacked in manpower during the late 1980s (as a result of the explosion in domestic demand that was one outcome of the speculative bubble), unlike Toyota no doubts were raised about its production system. In part, this was certainly due to its better working and employment conditions; and also to a mobility that was primarily based on employees' personal competency.

Honda's severest difficulties were related to the failure of several of its models. The company had believed that the rapid enriching of certain sections of the population (one result of the speculative bubble) would durably orient demand towards sporty and/or luxury cars, and it therefore built up the number of models it offered in this category. For as long as the speculative bubble lasted in the Triad countries, this appeared to be the right choice. In 1990, Honda's worldwide output was twice what it had been in 1979, reaching 1.94 million units. The company had become the world's eighth largest car maker, moving ahead of Chrysler and Renault. Half of its cars were sold in North America, 35 per cent in Japan, nine per cent in Europe and six per cent in the rest of the world. A half a million Hondas were being manufactured overseas.

However, once the speculative bubble burst and recession erupted in Japan, Honda's product policies were brutally invalidated. Realising the errors it had made regarding qualitative changes in demand, Honda reacted without delay. Whilst preparing to launch its own models, it began to market Land Rovers in Japan, as well as a restyled off-road Isuzu vehicle. The successful launch of a recreational vehicle (the CR-V) in 1996, and of a mini-van in 1997, contributed strongly to the resurgence in its sales. Its domestic output went back up to 1.31 million units in 1999, close to its historical peak of 1990 – despite the fact that its domestic market was still stagnating. That same year, Honda's global output reached 2.33 million vehicles.

The future for the `innovation and flexibility´ strategy and the Honda model

The relevancy of the 'innovation and flexibility' strategy has been reinforced by certain countries' recent tendency to develop a 'competitive' distribution of national income. This explains the extremely rapid renaissance of manufacturers such as Chrysler and Renault who have reverted to this strategy (or adopted it for the first time). Chrysler did this in the 1980s with its new line of SUV's – products that accounted for one-third of the American market by 1999. Renault adopted the strategy the 1990s, launching a complete range of passenger vans after noting the success of its initial top-of-the-range model. However, neither Chrysler nor Renault has been able so far to procure means that are coherent, and which will enable them to durably and profitably pursue an 'innovation and flexibility' strategy.

Chrysler in particular was not quick enough to acquire the indispensable financial independence, i.e., it could not lock up its shareholder structure. An attempted takeover in which Chrysler was a target for Kirk Kerkorian, a financier associated with one of the firm's former CEO's (Lee Iacocca), induced the firm's executives to agree to a merger with Daimler. However, the expected complementarity between the two firms turned out to be incompatibility – stemming from the fact that they had been pursuing different profit strategies. For the time being, not only has Chrysler gained nothing out of what has purely and simply turned into a takeover, but many projects involving innovative models have been abandoned and the company's main innovators, in a weakened position, have left it. By early 2002, Chrysler's strategy had lost all visibility. Renault, somewhat surprised by the success of its innovative models (which ended up accounting for most of the firm's profits even though they should have only been the icing on the cake), preferred to prioritise productive and commercial internationalisation, taking over Nissan, Dacia and Samsung instead of confirming its strategy and devising a suitable model.

Until now, Honda has kept well away from any acquisitions or mergers. To further its development, it would have to be able to pursue its strategy in each of the world's regions, meaning that it would have to design, with these regions in mind, models that satisfy the expectations of their new population sectors. It might decide to do this on its own or by arranging an alliance with a manufacturer that has shown itself capable of doing this, i.e., who is already pursuing the same strategy. Honda has chosen to follow the first path, one with which it has already been successful in North America.

9
Conclusion

The three industrial models that are commonly distinguished in the automobile sector and by extension in all industries ('craft production', 'mass production' and 'lean production') actually stem from historical amalgamations and conceptual confusions.

A re-evaluation of the history of productive models

By the beginning of the 20th century, most automobile firms had become industrial companies that relied upon machine tools and interchangeable parts (even when their vehicles were being built at stationary workstations or on short non-mechanised lines). Such firms did not disappear from the United States because they could not compete with the mass producers – the real reasons were the collapse in their specific clientele, and the cash problems they suffered from after the 1929 Depression. Not only did firms of this ilk survive in other countries, they even thrived, competing efficiently with Ford's overseas subsidiaries. It was these latter entities that, in the absence of those conditions that are propitious for mass consumption, could not remain profitable for long. Moreover, with the diverse product range these industrial companies offered, and because of the flexibility of their production system, they were able to function profitably in markets that were both limited and diversified. Towards this end, they built up several productive models, at least two of which have been identified and described: the Taylor and the Woollard models. Many analysts affirm that they have a sound understanding of the former, which they see as a forerunner of large series production – but they are wrong, given that in actual fact it was not towards this end that the model had actually been conceived.

Table 9.1   Productive models

| Models | Profit strategy being implemented | Company governance compromise | Components of the model | | | Dynamics |
			Product policy	Productive organisation	Employment relationship	Risks Contradictions
Taylor	Diversity and flexibility	High wages, inexpensive workforce, 'scientific' methods	Specific products, varied product offer, medium-sized series	Standard procedures and allocated times, flexibility of equipment and stationary individual workstations	Task-based wages, augmented by 30 to 100% if procedures followed and deadlines met	Conditional increases in productivity
Woollard	Diversity and flexibility	Autonomy and collective skills, flexibility, capital is well remunerated	Specific products, varied product offer, small & medium-sized series, lucrative price	Workshops for each product or subsystem, mechanisation and synchronisation of supplies	Autonomous teams, incentive-based piecework wages negotiated on a team-by-team basis	Establishment of a 'dual' management structure in the firm
Ford	Volume	Access to mass consumption vs. acceptance of productive organisation	Standard single product, drop in real prices	Production is integrated, continuous, mechanised, timed and broken down into elementary operations	Rising fixed wages, egalitarian, vs. parcellised and repetitive work	Rapid saturation of market, emergence of labour unions making demands

Sloan	Volume and diversity	Rising purchasing power vs. rising productivity	Hierarchised product range, shared platforms, superficial diversity, many options	Strategic centralisation and operational decentralisation, tools are polyvalent and subcontracting	Wages depend on job being done, versatility vs. acceptance of the organisation	Management structure is weighed down, excessive diversity, cannibalisation of products
Toyota	Permanent reduction of costs at constant volumes	Longevity for firm and for employees' and suppliers' jobs	Well-equipped basic models, good quality that is perceptible to the client	Polyvalent work team, 'Just-in-Time' inside and outside of firm	Employment and career guarantee vs. collective participation in reduction of standard times	Limits of social and political acceptability, severe competition in certain situations
Honda	Innovation and flexibility	Self-funded, individual promotion vs. responsiveness and initiative	Conceptually innovative and specific models, anticipation of customer expectations	Lines, machines and personnel can be quickly converted	Hiring, wages and promotions depend on initiative, expertise and responsiveness	Loss of innovation income because product is copied rapidly, loss of autonomy

Boyer, R., Freyssenet, M, GERPISA, 2002

Mass production, inaccurately labelled 'Taylor-Ford' production by some analysts, is in fact a mixture of two models, the 'Ford' and the 'Sloan', whose conditions of viability and characteristics diverge, even if they share with one other (and also with other models) mechanised production or assembly line principles. The Ford model implements a 'volume' strategy with its mass production of a standard vehicle, whereas the Sloan model implements a 'volume and diversity' strategy by 'superficially' diversifying models by body, internal fittings and accessories whilst commonalising non-visible parts and units. Just as the former model's existence was transitory and geographically limited, from the 1950s onwards the latter was seen as the one that everyone should be adopting, given the finely hierarchised demand that was developing from the bottom to the top-of-the-range. After all, this was an era marked by the clear convergence of these two segments.

Nevertheless, the Sloan model's diffusion was impeded by the crisis of work that broke out in the late 1960s – and then put to rest by the monetary and oil crises of 1971–1974. These crises even appeared to have killed off, once and for all, the model's entire viability. However, it was actually during the 1960s that the Sloan model first got into trouble in the United States, paradoxically as a result of its success, and even as it was being feted as a one best way for the second half of the 20th century. In addition, it did not spread as widely as people were predicting in the precipitously generalised managerial speeches of the time. In fact, it was only adopted by a few firms in those industrialised countries where national income distribution was being carried out in a co-ordinated and moderately hierarchised way.

Productive models are neither unique to a major historical era nor to a given country

Not one but two original industrial models were taking shape at the same time in the Japanese automobile industry: the Toyota model, with its emphasis on a 'permanent reduction in costs', and the Honda model, with its implementation of an 'innovation and flexibility' profit strategy. These two models have been wrongly amalgamated under the title of *'lean production'*, but in fact they differ on certain essential points. Moreover, the remarkable performances of the firms that have embodied these models, Toyota and Honda, did not spell the death of a Sloan model that Volkswagen began to adopt in 1974 (and with which Volkswagen profitably exploited the possibilities it faced in a market that found itself in a product renewal phase). In fact, these were the only three firms to have had a 'break even point' that was constantly and significantly below their value-added threshold. All other car makers' automobile businesses experienced periods of non-profitability.

These three firms' performances did not result from some intrinsic and timeless quality of the models they embodied. They stemmed first and foremost from the extent to which they had implemented profit strategies that suited the 'growth mode' of their countries of origin. Moreover, these growth modes turned out to be perfectly adapted to the new international circumstances that marked the post-1974 period. In undermining international growth, floating exchange rates and oil crises provoked a confrontation between industrialised economies. The countries that found themselves in a favourable position were those where growth was export-driven, and where a co-ordinated and moderately hierarchised distribution of national income was being carried out as a function of external competitiveness (i.e., Japan and West Germany). The firms that were particularly in tune with the new environment were those where the profit strategy was either based on a 'permanent reduction in costs' (like Toyota), on 'innovation and flexibility' (like Honda), or on 'volume and diversity' (like Volkswagen, which despite the sudden and durable slowdown in demand was again able to achieve economies of scale through a systematic commonalisation of the platforms used for its own models or for the models turned out by the manufacturers it was acquiring).

In addition to this first condition of profitability, the three companies also fulfilled the second one, developing a 'company governance compromise' between the main protagonists of their 'product policy', 'productive organisation' and 'employment relationship'. This is what enabled each of them to implement the strategy it had chosen with a modicum of coherency.

Certain Japanese car makers, notably Nissan, Mazda and Mitsubishi, either straddled several strategies or were unable to build a lasting compromise based upon coherent means. Starting in the 1980s, Japanese firms began to experience difficulties that observers at the time chose not to analyse as being the result of a 'Japanese model' they still considered to be superior. The 'quality' strategy of several German and Swedish manufacturers was particularly in tune with the 'co-ordinated and specialised export-oriented' growth mode being pursued in their respective countries. But they too were unable to adopt a durable company governance compromise (see table 9.2).

When growth models are destabilised, productive models must be rearranged

The countries where pre-1974 growth had been consumption-driven and where national income distribution was geared not towards external competitiveness but towards internal productivity gains (the United States, France, Italy plus 'competitive and competed' mode countries like Great Britain) were destabilised by the monetary and oil crises of the 1970s. It is noteworthy that all of these countries' car makers, without exception, experienced at least one major crisis between 1974 and 1990 – and that during this period none was able to rebuild, adopt or invent a productive model.

The international situation changed again during the 1990s. The liberalisation of capital movements during the late 1980s provoked a speculative bubble at first. In turn, this started to destabilise countries characterised by a 'co-ordinated and export-oriented' growth mode – as well as their top corporate performers. In 1990 Toyota experienced a deep-seated crisis of work that forced it to change its company governance compromise and to thoroughly transform its productive model. Honda was wrong about emerging demand. Volkswagen, carried on the wings of its own growth, found it difficult to control costs. Concomitantly, those car makers that had experienced difficulties in earlier times began to carry out drastic reorganisations and occasion-ally significant strategic re-orientations. The bursting of Japan's speculative bubble (Boyer, Yamada, 2000), Europe's restrictive budgetary policies, the emergence of certain countries and above all the transformation of growth modes subsequently changed the relationships between countries; the demand for automobiles; the nature of the labour that could be mobilised; and the geography of the automobile.

A number of industrialised countries began to develop a national income distribution that was more 'competitive' in nature, i.e., based on a local and category-specific balance of power and on financial opportunism. Directly or indirectly, they accentuated the destabilisation of those 'exporting' countries that for the most part had maintained a broadly co-ordinated and moderately hierarchised distribution. Countries' confrontations with one another thus changed in nature and in meaning.

It is in this context that the rearrangement of a world space that had been split up into several tendencies began. To this can be added the generalisation of trade liberalisation, the constitution of regional spaces

Table 9.2 Firms with durably high performances – and all the others: 1974–1990.

The internal and external conditions of profitability; the profit strategy's to the growth mode of national income; the company governance compromise's coherency with respect to the profit strategy being pursued

Growth mode of the national income	Co-ordinated and consumer-oriented	Co-ordinated and export oriented		Competitive and competed
		Specialised	Price	
Viability following 1971—1974 monetary and oil crises	In crisis	Helped		Instability is accentuated
Countries	United States, France, Italy	Germany, Sweden	Japan, Korea	Great Britain
Firms that performed best				
Relevant strategy and coherent company governance compromise				
Productive models – Sloan – Toyota – Honda		VW	Toyota Honda	
Firms that have experienced a crisis				
Profit strategy not relevant to growth mode	Citroën (1974)			BLMC-Rover (1974, 1986)
Company governance compromise that are incoherent	Ford (1979) Chrysler (1980) Fiat (1980) PSA (1982) Renault (1984) General Motors (1985)	Volvo (1984, 1990) Saab (1990) Mercedes (1990) BMW (1990)	Mazda (1974–1979) Mitsubishi (1974) Hyundaï (1985) Nissan (1986)	

Boyer, R., Freyssenet, M., GERPISA, 2002

Note: The year of the financial crisis of each firm is shown in parentheses

and the reaffirmation or affirmation of nations, whether 'emerging' or not.

The liberalisation of capital movements gave shareholders back a role that they had not assumed for many years. They tried to wield as much of their new influence as possible in such a way as to forge new company governance compromises and thus shape new productive models.

'Competitive' distributions of income, through the economic and social disparities that they engendered, also gave birth to a second automobile market for pickup trucks, minivans, recreational vehicles and other conceptually innovative means of transport. This second market, which in the United States in particular has become just as large as the market for saloon cars, has given a new and broader relevancy to the 'innovation and flexibly' strategy that firms like Chrysler and Renault have adopted, following Honda's example. As such, automobile firms are having to make bets nowadays on which global rearrangement will prevail, and on which growth mode will carry the day. This has important consequences for the relevancy of their profit strategies and for the company governance compromises that they will be able to preserve, rebuild or invent.

The two conditions underlying firms´ longevity: relevancy and coherency

Given recent research efforts, new representations of the industrial history of the automobile are a long way away from offering the previous representation's touching simplicity, with its tenet that three successive models have each constituted the one best way of their respective eras. Yet does this mean that firms' players (shareholders, banks, owners, executives, employees, labour unions, suppliers, etc.) are entirely lacking in common ground? If diversity is omnipresent, how is it possible to choose a productive model that is economically relevant yet socially acceptable in differing environments? Why is it that certain firms have been unable to embody or to invent any model whatsoever, or else have gone through long periods of oscillation between profit and losses (and even disappeared)?

Contrary to appearances, this more complex and broader vision of the history of the automobile sector has helped us to come up with rules that are general and valid at all times and in all places – and which in any event are much more operational (at both an analytical and at a practical level) than rules which simply consist of affirming that only one model can perform well in a given era (with their naïve suggestion that this model should be adopted lock, stock and barrel by anyone concerned). GERPISA's analysis of firms' trajectories enables us to highlight the two essential conditions of profitability – and to delineate the room to manoeuvre that these conditions afford a firm's players to invent or else to adopt forms of production that can lead to a compromise which is acceptable to all.

What can a firm's players do?

The invention of a productive model is not only a matter of willingness and intelligence. It first implies a synchronisation of those conditions that turn the chosen profit strategy into something that is viable – and which enable those means that will allow for its implementation. Players generally have no control, whether at a cognitive or at a practical level, over this synchronisation. Very often it is only afterwards that they realise which conditions and means are beginning to constitute a system, and that they make efforts to reinforce this process and to theorise it.

Similarly, the adoption of a model that has proven itself elsewhere is more than just a simple exercise in intellectual conversion and/or an application of well-established systems. Players can never be sure that their decisions will actually allow for a synchronisation of conditions and means, given the many social processes that are involved and the difficulty of foreseeing their inter-relationships.

The practical utility of research and of social science is specifically that they help to identify social processes, clarifying their entanglement, highlighting potential room to manoeuvre and helping the various agents involved to act in a manner that is coherent with their own outlook.

The two main conditions of a firm's profitability

1. The relevancy of the 'profit strategy' to the 'growth modes' of the countries in which the firm is operating

2. The solidity of the 'company governance compromise' that enables the firm's players to discover and to implement those means (product policy, productive organisation and employment relationship) that are both coherent with the profit strategy that has been adopted and also acceptable to them – in other words, the ability to invent or to adopt a 'productive model'.

Companies are mortal. This was overlooked by a generation that lived in the post-war boom environment of generally rising living standards and upwards social mobility. Many executives, employees and union representatives did not know what to do when faced with crises that previous methods, whether driven by management or by the unions, could not resolve in a way that satisfied people's expectations and hopes.

Given the analytical framework this book has developed, we can say that to protect oneself from such situations and to support their political and social perspectives, a firm's players can theoretically act on the national 'growth mode', the 'profit strategy' that has been chosen and the contents of the 'company governance compromise'. But as we have seen, the ability to act varies greatly for each of these.

First of all, countries are not totally free to choose their growth mode. In addition to their specific resources and history, the choice is subject to their international relationships, particularly their ties with the hegemonic country of the time. A consumption-driven growth and a co-ordinated and moderately hierarchised distribution of national income is only possible if customs barriers or structural advantages shelter a country from more competitive foreign products. Yet a country has to negotiate with other countries when defining its customs regime. The growth mode's determination, something that conditions the various profit strategies' relevancy (i.e., the first condition of profitability), is thus more or less totally out of the hands of the firm's players. It is much harder for them to have their national growth mode maintained or changed so that it remains or becomes suitable for their profit strategy – and much easier to change their product strategy so that it becomes relevant.

However, players cannot remain passive. Each has his/her own objectives and vision of the future. Each may wish that one or the other mode be maintained or established, depending on his/her view, for example, of national sovereignty, or of the proper distribution of the wealth being created. There are historical circumstances where action is not only possible but necessary, i.e., after a war, between 1974 and 1980, or in all likelihood at the dawn of this new century – in other words, whenever previous growth modes have been destabilised and/or when several options exist.

A firm's players can theoretically choose amongst those profit strategies that have been enabled by the growth modes that are present in the places where the firm is operating. Of course, such choices cannot be made freely, far from it. They depend on the product strategy that the firm is already applying, and on other manufacturers' profit strategies. A change in profit strategies cannot be decreed from above. It requires first of all rebuilding the company governance compromise which governs the means that are to be applied, hence a commitment to a long and potentially conflicting process whose outcome is never assured. It then depends on how much room one's competitors have left for a choice to be made. It may be risky to adopt the same strategy as them, given that they are already in business and have built a solid company governance compromise (one that creates synergies between the means they are using). All that remains then is to choose one profit strategy out of all of those that are rendered feasible by the national growth mode – a strategy that has to a certain extent been left untouched. Yet there are also circumstances where it is feasible and even necessary to invent a new strategy, one that creates compatibility between sources of profit previously considered to be contradictory. One example is volume and diversity, two strategies made compatible by General Motors during the interwar period.

History moves forward

It is clearly in the building of a company governance compromise that a firm's players dispose of the greatest room to manoeuvre. But it is still crucial that executives (who often operate under time constraints, notably during crisis periods) avoid declaiming that no solution exists other than the one they have designed. An analysis of automobile companies' trajectories over the past century tells us that this is the best way to never become durably profitable. All the company governance compromises that have led to the invention or adoption of a productive model have required at least ten years, plus an intelligent understanding amongst the firm's partners, to ensure that none have been forced to renege their personal convictions or objectives.

In the late 1990s, American firms were exploring a new productive paradigm based on information technologies, productive internationalisation and high yields for invested capital. For many analysts, information technology means that the type of modular production that was observed in the electronics industry will soon generalise to all sectors. Regarding the automobile, aside from the fact that ICT usage is being superimposed on the sector's own innovation trajectory, it has not per se had any determinant effects. It will be deployed, as was the case with automation, in a very differentiated manner, depending on the profit strategies and productive models involved. For example, ICT can be used to develop competition between suppliers in the Sloan and Honda models, or to organise cost-cutting in the Toyota model.

Productive internationalisation carries with it a far greater potential for change. This is because growth modes, far from converging as certain observers have repeatedly claimed, have in fact been re-diversifying. The tensions between the requirements of a firm's strategy and the social and economic space within which the firm is established are likely to foster, through a hybridisation process, the emergence of unprecedented configurations, these being the embryos of new and fully fledged productive models.

The rise of the financial sphere will definitely have an effect on the government compromise in those firms that do not have any control over their own shareholders or funding mechanisms. However, the same will not necessarily apply to car makers such as Toyota or Honda, since they have been able to preserve their financial independence, as befits the requirements of their own profit strategy.

The euphoria that was provoked by the wave of mergers–acquisitions–alliances in the automobile industry during the late 1990s is starting to give way to a more realistic evaluation of the ever-renewed diversity of productive models.

Bibliography

Abernathy, W. J., Clark, K. B., Kantrow, A. M. (1983) *Industrial Renaissance. Producing a Competitive Future for America*, New York: Basic Books.

Aglietta M. (1976) *Régulation et crise du capitalisme: l'expérience des États-Unis*, Paris: Calmann-Lévy.

Aoki, M. (1988) *Information, Incentives and Bargaining in the Japanese Economy*, Cambridge: Cambridge University Press.

Babson, S. (ed.) (1995) *Lean Work. Empowerment and Exploitation in the Global Auto Industry*, Detroit: Wayne State University Press

Bardou, J. P., Chanaron, J. J., Fridenson P. and Laux J. M. (1982) *The Automobile Revolution*, Chapel Hill.

Berggren, C. (1992) *Alternatives to Lean Production: Work Organisation in the Swedish Auto Industry*, New York: ILR

Bigazzi, D. (2000) 'Mass Production Orrganized Craftmanship? the Post-War Italian Automobile Industry' in Zeitlin, J., Herrigel, G., eds *Americanization and its Limits. Reworking US Technology and Management in Post-War Europe and Japan*, Oxford: Oxford University Press.

Briggs, L, (1996) *The Rational Factory: Architecture, Technology and Work in America's Age of Mass Production*, Baltimore: The John Hopkins University Press.

Boyer, R., Mistral, J. (1978) *Accumulation, Inflation et Crise*, Paris: PUF.

Boyer, R. (dir.), (1986) *Capitalisme fin de siècle*, Paris: PUF

Boyer, R. (ed.) (1988) *The Search for Labour Market Flexibility*, Oxford: Clarendon.

Boyer, R. (1990) *The Regulation School: a Critical Introduction*, New York: Columbia University Press.

Boyer, R., Freyssenet, M. (1995) 'Emergence of New Industrial Models: Hypothesis and Analysis Procedure'. In *Actes du GERPISA*, 15.

Boyer, R. (1996) 'The Convergence Hypothesis Revisited: Globalization but still the Century of Nations? in Berger, S., Dore, R. (eds), *National Diversity and Global Capitalism*, Ithaca: Cornell University Press.

Boyer, R, Durand, J. P. (1997) *After Fordism*, London: Macmillan.

Boyer, R., Charron E., Jurgens U. and Tolliday S. (eds) (1998) *Between Imitation and Innovation: the Transfer and Hybridization of Productive Models in the International Automobile Industry*, Oxford: Oxford University Press.

Boyer R., Yamada T. (eds) (2000) *Japanese Capitalism in Crisis*, London: Routledge

Boyer R., Saillard Y. (eds) (2001) *Regulation Theory: the State of Art*, London: Routledge

Boyer, R., Freyssenet, M. (forthcoming) *The World that Changed the Machine*.

Bravermann, H. (1974) *Labor and Monopoly Capital*, New York: Monthly Review Press.

Chandler, A. D. (1964) *Ford, General Motors and the Automobile Industry*, New York: Harcourt.

Church, R. (1994) *The Rise and Decline of the British Motor Industry*, London: Macmillan.

Comacchio, A., Volpato, G., Camuffo, A. (eds) (1999) *Automation in Automotive Industries: Recent Development*, Berlin: Springer.

Cusumano, M. (1985) *The Japanese Automobile Industry: Technology & Management at Nissan & Toyota*, Cambridge, Mass.: Harvard University Press.

De Montmollin, M., Pastré, O., Dir. (1984) *Le Taylorisme*, Paris: La Découiverte.

Durand, J. P., Stewart, P., Castillo, J. J. (eds) (1998) *Teamwork in the Automobile Industry. Radical Change or Passing Fashion*, London: Macmillan.

Ellegard, K., Engström, T., Nilsson, L. (1991) *Reforming Industrial Work: Principles and Realities*, Stockholm: Arbetsmiljöfonden.

Flinck, J. J. (1989) *The Automobile Age*, Cambridge, Mass.: MIT Press.

Ford, H. (1922) *My Life and Work*, Doubleday.

Ford, H. (1926) *Today and Tomorrow*, Doubleday.

Foreman-Peck, J., Bowden, S., Mckinlay, A. (1995) *The British Motor Industry*, Manchester: Manchester University Press.

Freyssenet, M. (1974) *La division capitaliste du travail.*, Paris: Savelli.

Freyssenet, M. (1984) 'Division du travail, taylorisme et automatisation: confusions, différences et enjeux', in De Montmolin, M. Pastré, O., *Le Taylorisme*, Paris: La Découverte.

Freyssenet, M. (1997) 'The Current Social Form of Automation and a Conceivable Alternative: French Experience', in Shimokawa, K. et al. (eds) *Transforming Automobile Assembly: Experience in Automation and Work Organization*, Springer: Berlin.

Freyssenet M. (1998a) 'Reflective Production: An Alternative to Mass-Production and to Lean Production?', in *Economic and Industrial Democracy*, Vol. 19, No. 1.

Freyssenet, M., Mair, A., Shimizu, K., Volpato, G. (eds) (1998b) *One Best Way? Trajectories and Industrial Models of World's Automobile Producers*, Oxford: Oxford University Press.

Freyssenet, M (1998c) 'Intersecting Trajectories and Model Changes', in Freyssenet, M., et al. (eds) *One Best Way? Trajectories and Industrial Models of the World's Automobile Producers.*, Oxford: Oxford University Press.

Freyssenet, M. (1999a) 'Competitive Strategies, Industrial Models and Assembly Automation Templates', in Comacchio, A., et al. (eds) *Automation in Automotive Industries: Recents Developements*, Springer: Berlin.

Freyssenet, M. (1999b) 'Emergence, Centrality and End of Work', in *Current Sociology*, 1999, Vol. 47, No. 2.

Freyssenet, M., Lung, Y. (2000) 'Between Globalisation and Regionalisation: What is the Future of the Motor Industry', in Humphrey, J., Lecler, Y., Salerno, M. S. (eds) *Global Strategies and Local Realities: the Auto Industry in Emerging Markets*, London: Macmillan; New York: St Martin's Press.

Fridenson, P. (1972) *Histoire des usines Renault: Naissance de la grande industrie, 1898–1939*, Paris: Le Seuil.

Fridenson, P. (1982) 'Diffusion of the Revolution', in Bardou, J. P. et al., *The Automobile Revolution*, Chapel Hill.

Fujimoto, T. (1999) the *Evolution of a Manufacturing System at Toyota*, Oxford: Oxford University Press.

Friedmann, G. (1936) *Problèmes humains du machinisme industriel*, Paris: Gallimard.

Glimsted, H. (1995) 'Non-Fordist Routes to Modernisation: Production, Innovation and the Political Construction of Markets in the Swedish Automobile Industry before 1960', in *Business and Economic History*.

Hounshell D. A. (1984): *From the American System to Mass Production, the Development of Manufacturing Technology in the United States, 1800–1932*, Baltimore: Johns Hopkins University Press.

Jetin, B. 'The Historical Evolution of Supply Variety: an International Comparative Study' in Lung, Y. et al., eds (1999) *Coping with Variety: Flexible Productive Systems for Product Variety in the Auto Industry*, London: Ashgate.

Kochan, T. A., Katz, H. C., Mckersie R. B. (1994) *The Transformation of American Industrial Relations*, New York.

Kuhn, A. J. (1986) *GM Passes Ford: 1918–1938*, University Park and London: The Pennsylvania State University Press.

Laux, J. (1982) Origin of a Revolution', in Bardou, J. P. et al., *The Automobile Revolution*, Chapel Hill.

Laux, J. (1992) *The European Automobile Industry*, New York: Twayne Publishers.

Lewchuk, W. (1987) *American Technology and the British Vehicle Industry*, New York: Cambridge University Press.

Lewchuk, W. (1989) 'Fordism and the Moving Assembly Line: the British and American Experience', in Lichtenstein, N. and Meyer, S., *On the Line: Essays in the History of Auto Work*, Chicago: University of Illinois Press.

Lichtenstein, N., Meyer, S. (1989) *On the Line.: Essays On the History of Auto Work*, Chicago: University of Illinois Press.

Linhart, R. (1976) *Lénine, Taylor et les paysans*, Paris: Le Seuil.

Loubet, J. L. (1995) *Citroën, Peugeot, Renault et les autres*, Paris: Le Monde-Editions.

Lung, Y., Chanaron, J. J., Fujimoto, T., Raff, D. (eds) (1999) *Coping with Variety: Flexible Productive Systems for Product Variety in the Auto Industry*, London: Ashgate.

Mair, A. (1994a) *Honda's Global Local Corporation*, London: Macmillan.

Mair, A. (1998) 'From BLMC to Rover Group: the Search for a Viable British Model', in Freyssenet et al., *One Best Way? Trajectories and Industrial Models of World's Automobile Producers*, Oxford: Oxford University Press.

Mayo, E. (1933) *Human Problems of an Industrial Civilization*, New York: Macmillan.

Meyer, S. (1981) 'The Persistence of Fordism: Workers and Technology in the American Automobile Industry', in Lichtenstein, N. and Meyer, S., *On the Line: Essays in the History of Auto Work*, Chicago: University of Illinois Press, 1989.

Meyer, S. (1981) *The Five-Dollar Day: Labor Management and Social Control in the Ford Motor Company, 1908–1921*, Albany: State University of New York Press.

Mishina, K. (1998) 'Revealing the Essence of Toyota's Manufacturing Capability: the Kentucky Transplant, 1986–1994' in Boyer et al., *Between Imitation and Innovation: the Transfer and Hybridization of Productive Models in the International Automobile Industry*, Oxford: Oxford University Press.

Mito, S. (1990) *The Honda Book of Management*, London: The Athlone Press.

Moutet, A. (1992): La rationalisation industrielle dans l'économie française: 1900–1939, Nanterre: Thèse d'État.

Nelson, D. (1975) *Managers and Workers: Origins of the New Factory System in the United States, 1880–1920*, Madison: The University of Wisconsin Press.

Nelson, D. (1980) *Frederick W. Taylor, the Rise of Scientific Management*, Madison: The University of Wisconsin Press.

Nevins, A., Hill, F. E. (1957) *Ford, Expansion and Challenge, 1915–1933*, New York: Scribners.

Nevins, A., Hill, F. E. (1963) *Ford: Decline and Rebirth 1933–1962*, New York: Scribners.

Nilsson, L. (1995) 'The Uddevalla Plant: Why did it Succeed with a Holistic Approach and why did it Come to an End?', in Ake Sandberg (ed.) *Enriching Production*, Avebury: Aldershot.

Ohno, T. (1990) *L'esprit Toyota*, Paris: Masson.

Ohno, T. (1993) *Présent et avenir du toyotisme*, Paris: Masson

Piore M., Sabel Ch. (1984): *The Second Industrial Divide*, New York: Basic Books

Porter, M. E. (1985) *The Competitive Advantage*, New York: The Free Press.

Raff, D. (1998) 'Models, Trajectories, and the Evolution of Production Systems: Lessons from the American Automobile Industry in the Years between the Wars' in Freyssenet, et al. (eds) *One Best Way? Trajectories and Industrial Models of the World's Automobile Producers*, Oxford: Oxford University Press.

Raff, D. (1999) 'G.M. and the Evolving Industrial Organisation of American Automobile Manufacturing in the Interwar Years', in Lung et al. eds, *Coping with Variety: Flexible Productive Systems for Product Variety in the Auto Industry*, London: Ashgate.

Roos, D., Altshuler, A. (eds) (1985) *The Future of the Automobile*, Cambridge, Mass.: MIT Press.

Sakiya, T. (1990) *Honda Motor: The Men, the Management, the Machines*, New York: Kodansha International.

Sandberg, A. (Ed) (1995) *Enriching Production*, Avebury: Aldershot.

Sanders, S. (1975) *Honda, the Man and His Machines*, Boston: Little Brown.

Shimizu, K. (1998) A New Toyotaism? in Freyssenet et al., (eds) *One Best Way? Trajectories and Industrial Models of the World's Automobile Producers*, Oxford: Oxford University Press.

Shimizu, K. (1999) *Le Toyotisme*, Paris: Repères, La Découverte.

Shimokawa, K. (1994) *The Japanese Automobile Industry, a Business History*, London: The Athlone Press.

Shimokawa, S., Jurgens, U., Fujimoto, T. (1997) *Transforming Automobile Industry: Experience in Automation and Work Organisation*, Berlin: Springer

Shiomi, H., Wada, K. (eds) (1995) *Fordism Transformed: the Development of Production Methods in the Automobile Industry*, Oxford: Oxford University Press.

Shook, R. L. (1988) *Honda: an American Success Story*, Prentice Hall: New York.

Sloan, A. P. (1963) *My Years With General Motors*, New York: Doubleday and Currency.

Sorensen, C. (1962) *My Forty Years With Ford*, Collier Books.

Streeck, W. (1992) *Social Institutions and Economic Performance*, London: Sage.

Taylor, F. W. (1902) 'Shop Management', in *American Society of Mechanical Engineers*, Vol. 24.

Taylor, F. W. (1911) *Principles of Scientific Management*, New York: Harper and Brother.

Tolliday, S. (1998a) 'The Diffusion and Transformation of Fordism: Britain and Japan Compared', in Boyer et al. (eds) *Between Imitation and Innovation: the Transfer and Hybridization of Productive Models in the International Automobile Industry*, Oxford: Oxford University Press.

Tolliday, S. (1998b) *The Rise and the Fall of Mass Production*, Cheltenham: Edward Elgar.

Tolliday, S., Zeitlin, J. (eds) (1991) *The Power to Manage: Employers and Industrial Relations in Comparative-Historical Perspective*, London: Routledge.

Tolliday, S., Zeitlin, J. (eds) (1992) *Between Fordism and Flexibility: the Automobile Inustry and its Workers*, Oxford: Berg.

Touraine, A. (1955) *L'évolution du travail ouvrier aux usines Renault*, Paris: Ed. du CNRS.

Volpato G. (1983) *L'industria automobilistica internazionale*, Padua: Cedam.

White, L. J. (1971) *The Automobile Industry since 1945*, Cambridge, Mass.: Harvard University Press.

Williams, K., Haslam, C., Johal S. and Williams, J. (1994) *Cars: Analysis, History, Cases*, Oxford: Berghahm.

Womack J., Jones D. T., Roos D. (1990) *The Machine that Changed the World*, New York: Macmillan.

Woollard, F. (1924) 'Some Notes on British Methods of Continuous Production', *Proceedings of the Institution of Automobile Engineers*, Vol. 19.

Woollard, F. (1954) *Principles of Mass and Flow Production*, London: Iliffe.

Zeitlin, J. (1999) *Between Flexibility and Mass Production: Strategic Debate and Industrial Reorganisation in British Engineering, 1830–1999*, Oxford: Oxford University Press.

Zeitlin, J., Herrigel, G. (eds) (2000) *Americanization and its Limits: Reworking US Technology and Management in Post-War Europe and Japan*, Oxford: Oxford University Press.

GERPISA PUBLICATIONS

GERPISA edits in English and in French a quarterly review entitled *Actes du GERPISA* and a monthly newsletter called *La Lettre du GERPISA*. The review combines the writings that the network's members have presented on a specific topic in various work meetings. The newsletter comments upon news from the automotive world and provides up-to-date information on what is happening in the network. Findings from the first and second programmes have been published in a series of books:

Programme: `Emergence of new industrial models'

Freyssenet, M., Mair, A., Shimizu, K., Volpato, G. (eds), *One Best Way? Trajectories and Industrial Models of the World's Automobile Producers*, Oxford: Oxford University Press, 1998. French translation: *Quel modèle productif? Trajectoires et modèles industriels des constructeurs automobiles mondiaux*, Paris: La Découverte: 2000.

Boyer, R., Charron, E., Jürgens, U., Tolliday, S. (eds), *Between Imitation and Innovation: The Transfer and Hybridization of Productive Models in the International Automobile Industry*, Oxford: Oxford University Press, 1998.

Durand, J. P., Stewart, P., Castillo, J. J. (eds), *Teamwork in the Automobile Industry. Radical Change or Passing Fashion*, London: Macmillan, 1999. French translation: *L'avenir du travail à la chaîne*, Paris: La Découverte, 1998.

Lung, Y., Chanaron, J. J., Fujimoto, T., Raff, D. (eds), *Coping with Variety: Product Variety and Production Organization in the World Automobile Industry*, Aldershot: Ashgate, 1999.

Shimizu, K., *Le Toyotisme*, Repères, Paris: La Découverte, 1999.

Boyer, R., Freyssenet, M., *Les modèles productifs*, Paris: La Découverte, 2000. English translation: *Productive Models*, London and New York: Palgrave, 2002.

Boyer, R., Freyssenet, M., *The World that Changed the Machine* (forthcoming).

Programme: 'The automobile industry between globalisation and regionalisation'

Humphrey, J., Lecler, Y., Salerno, M. (eds), *Global Strategies and Local Realities: The Auto industry in Emerging Markets*, Basingstoke: Macmillan, and New York: St Martin's Press, 2000.

Freyssenet, M. Shimizu, K., Volpato, G. (eds), *Globalisation or Regionalisation? International Trajectories of the Automobile Industry Companies* (forthcoming).

Carillo, J., Lung, Y., Van Tulder, R. (eds), *Cars ... Carriers of Regionalism* (forthcoming).

Programme: 'Co-ordination of knowledge and competencies in the regional automotive systems'

Lung, Y. and Volpato, G. (eds), 'Reconfiguring the Auto Industry", *International Journal of Automotive Technology and Management* (IJTAM), vol. 2, no. 1, 2000.

Williams, K. (ed.), 'The tyranny of finance? New agendas for auto research', *Competition and Change*, vol. 6, double issue nos. 1 and 2, 2002.

Appendix: GERPISA International Network

Permanent Group for the Study of and Research into the Automobile
Industry and its Employees

École des Hautes Études en Sciences Sociales, Paris

Université d'Évry Val d'Essonne

GERPISA (Permanent Group for the Study of and Research into the Automobile Industry and its Employees) started out as a network of French economics, management, history and sociology researchers who were interested in the automobile industry. Founded by Michel Freyssenet (CNRS sociologist) and Patrick Fridenson (EHESS historian), it was transformed into an international network in 1992 in order to carry out a research programme on the 'Emergence of new industrial models'.

With Robert Boyer (CEPREMAP, CNRS, EHESS economist) and Michel Freyssenet supervising its scientific orientations and under the management of an international committee, the programme (which lasted from 1993 to 1996) made it possible, thanks to its study of the automobile firms' (and their transplants') trajectories, productive organisation and employment relationships, to demonstrate that lean production, which according to the authors of *The machine that Changed the World* was supposed to become the industrial model of the 21st century, was in fact an inaccurate amalgamation of two completely different productive models, the 'Toyota' and the 'Honda'. Moreover, it showed that there are, have always been, and probably always will be several productive models that are capable of performing well at any one time. Shareholders, executives and employees are not only not obliged to adopt a one best way, they have to devise a 'company governance compromise' covering the means that will allow them to implement one of the several profit strategies that are relevant to the economic and social environment in which they find themselves.

A second programme (running from 1997 to 1999) entitled 'The Automobile Industry, between Globalisation and Regionalisation' and supervised by Michel Freyssenet and by Yannick Lung (Bordeaux IV, economist), tested the analytical framework that had been developed during the first programme in an attempt to better understand the new wave of car manufacturer and components maker internationalisation that had been observed over the previous decade. The outcome was that the viability of the choices being made depends primarily on the chosen profit strategies' compatibility with the growth modes in the spaces being invested.

The third programme (2000–2002) is currently being developed under Yannick Lung's supervision. It focuses on the issues at stake in the 'Coordination of Knowledge and Competencies in the Regional Automotive Systems'. Supplementing existing studies of forms of regionalisation in the automobile industry, the programme analyses the sector's new contours as well as the development of new relational and co-operative modes amongst its players.

In 2000, the GERPISA counted 350 members from 27 different countries. Affiliated with the Centre de Recherches Historiques (CRH) of the Ecole des Hautes Etudes en Sciences Sociales (EHESS) and acknowledged as a host structure by the French Ministry of National Education, its administrative offices are located in the Université d'Evry. It receives additional financial and material support from the French car companies, from their professional association (the CCFA), and from the European Union.

The international management committee is comprised of 24 members: Annie Beretti (Innovation Department, PSA), Robert Boyer (CNRS-EHESS, Paris) Juan José Castillo (Universidad Complutense, Madrid) Jorge Carrillo (Colegio de la Frontera Norte, Mexique), Jean-Jacques Chanaron (CNRS, Lyon), Elsie Charron (CNRS, Paris), Jean-Pierre Durand (Université d'Evry), Michel Freyssenet (CNRS, Paris), Patrick Fridenson (EHESS, Paris), Takairo Fujimoto (University of Tokyo), John Humphrey (Sussex University), Bruno Jetin (Université Paris XIII), Ulrich Jurgens (WZB, Berlin), Yveline Lecler (MRASH/IAO, Lyon), Yannick Lung (Université de Bordeaux IV), Jean-Claude Monnet (Research Department, Renault), Mario Sergio Salerno (University of São Paolo), Koichi Shimizu (University of Okayama), Koichi Shimokawa (Hosei University, Tokyo), Paul Stewart (Cardiff University), Steve Tolliday (Leeds University), Rob Van Tulder (Erasmus University, Rotterdam), Giuseppe Volpato (Ca'Foscari University in Venise), Karel Williams (Victoria University, Manchester).

Information on GERPISA's activities can be obtained by contacting GERPISA réseau international. Université d'Évry-Val d'Essonne.
4 Boulevard François Mitterrand, 91025 Evry cedex, France
Phone: 33 (1) 69 47 70 23 – Fax 33 (1) 69.47.80.35
E-mail: contact@gerpisa.univ-evry.fr
Website: http//www.gerpisa.univ-evry.fr

Index